SURF LESSONS

Stories Of An Eastern Surfer

Earl Shores

Books by Earl Shores

The Unforgettable Buzz: The History of Electric Football and Tudor Games

"The Unforgettable Buzz is a thoroughly researched and cleverly written study of electric football. Every Baby Boomer who played the game - and that's all of us - will love this book."
— *Ray Didinger, Pro Football Hall of Fame Sportswriter and NFL Films Emmy® Award Winning Writer and Producer*

Full Color Electric Football ™

"More than a nostalgic nod to a much loved game, Full Color Electric Football deftly documents the rise of pro football, the equally innovative (and competitive) path of iconic toy companies like Tudor, whose evolution changed their game as much as, say, the no huddle offense shifted the NFL's gears."
— *Reuben Jackson, author, poet, Host of Vermont Public Radio's Friday Night Jazz, former Curator of the Duke Ellington Collection at the Smithsonian in Washington, DC*

For Robin and Andy

First Edition, 2016

ISBN: 978-0-9892363-4-8

Library of Congress Control Number: 2016908138

One Way Road Press
P.O. Box 371
Media, PA 19063
onewayroadpress.com

Cover and logo design by Michael Kronenberg
Cover photo by Robin Huntington Shores
Title page art by Chris Tousimis

CONTENTS

SURF LESSONS

March 1979, Cape Hatteras, North Carolina

INTRODUCTION

The first words I ever put to paper with any serious intent were about surfing. And the term "put to paper" is more than just worn out literary jargon, as those first words were, in fact, scribbled onto a yellow legal pad. My goal was simple. I wanted to be published in *Surfer* magazine, the unquestioned voice of the surfing world. It seemed like I hit the lottery when the second story I ever sent them got a thumbs up from the editor. Wow, that wasn't hard...was it?

Well, that was 1992, and all these years later it's still a dream deferred. Diluting the disappointment, at least with several decades of distance, is the fact that I had an extended relationship with then *Surfer* Editor Steve Hawk. He liked my work and encouraged me to keep writing and submitting. As an unpublished writer I really couldn't have asked for anything more from an editor – other than to publish one of my stories.

While waiting for my *Surfer* debut a brand new magazine appeared here on the East Coast. It was called *Eastern Surf Magazine*, and was unique right from the start because it was a freebie. Every other month piles of *Eastern Surf* appeared in surf shops up and down the East Coast, and you could just walk in and grab a copy – or two, or three, or five. The earliest issues were black-and-white all photo affairs, with the majority of the photos coming from breaks along the East Coast. While the photos were excellent, and it was cool to see eastern surfers surfing eastern spots, what really stuck out was the juvenile attitude oozing from the magazine's pages. There were f-bomb ads, f-bombs in letters, revealing bikini photo features...all I could think was, if Beavis and Butt-Head ran a surf mag, this is what it would look like.

Then *Eastern Surf* put out an open call for stories to fill their "Talkin' Story" column. Figuring I had nothing to lose, off to Indialantic, Florida went a story that had received high marks but a "no thanks" from *Surfer*. I was sure *Eastern Surf* would love it. I knew the story was solid. And Steve Hawk's reason for rejecting it even looked like a seal of approval. He thought the story was "too East Coast."

Eastern Surf's response came in the form a handwritten note on copy machine letterhead, thoroughly lukewarm in tone, saying that while, yeah, the story was kind of cool, they really were looking for something grungier. If I wanted to grunge up my story and send it back, they'd be happy to take another look at it.

I was speechless...and completely pissed off. Grungy? You want grungy?

Who in the hell was this guy, anyway? My first thought was to send him my *Surfer* acceptance letter and say thanks, but no thanks, I'll soon be published in a *real* surf magazine. But after cooling off a bit I realized that I was in no position to burn any editorial bridges. Instead, I focused my anger and wrote the story of my worst-ever surfing experience, which up until that point, I had no desire to write about.

I didn't have to dig very deep to find a dark side, as the events of the story were plenty dark on their own, even to the termination of a friendship. I left the f-bombs in, as I did the bourbon, the marijuana, the pre-dawn puke session, and the "borrowed" motel blankets that were never returned. There was little question that my writing boundaries expanded as I channeled my inner T.C. Boyle. But I took the piece seriously, rewriting obsessively until I found 800 concise words to convey my still visceral disappointment from this unpleasant outing.

I was proud of the story – even if it was something that mom probably didn't need to read. In the mail it went, and frankly, whatever *Eastern Surf* thought…well, whatever.

Coming back from *Eastern Surf* was a hand-written three-page response, full of capital letters and exclamation points praising my story. It was written by Dick "Mez" Meseroll, who besides being the co-founder and editor of *Eastern Surf*, was (and still is) one of the most talented surf photographers ever to pick up a telephoto lens.

Mez published my story "Trick Or Treat" in the fall of 1993 (page 31). It was my breakthrough into the world of print, and it really was, to borrow a phrase, the "beginning of a beautiful friendship." Over the next two years my contributions to *Eastern Surf* reached double figures, as Mez even put my name on the magazine's masthead as a Contributing Writer. Something else Mez did was let me expand my work beyond his initial grungy requirements. This expansion, in addition to being able to pitch that I was a Contributing Writer at *Eastern Surf Magazine*, helped me land surf-inspired stories beyond the surf world, including in publications like *Highlights For Children*, the *Washington Post*, and the *Philadelphia Inquirer*.

Getting into these publications pushed my writing career from aspiring to established, and moved me beyond the niche of surf writer. The confidence and experience acquired in those early days laid the foundation for all that came afterward in my writing, including a 600-page book in 2013 (*The Unforgettable Buzz: The History of Electric Football and Tudor Games*).

But writing about surfing is where it all started. It's something I still love doing, and I think it's where I've done my best work. So I'm thrilled for the opportunity in *Surf Lessons* to put my surf stories together all in one place. They span the entire length of my surfing and writing career, and have been left in their time without any updating. A number of the pieces are from the *Eastern Surf* canon, while most of the others have their own story of how they just missed getting into print. "Summer School," for example, is the story that Steve Hawk and *Surfer* accepted back in 1992. It finally gets its long awaited debut here in *Surf Lessons* (page 7).

What I hope comes across throughout *Surf Lessons* is my passion for surfing. The sport has had a major impact on my life, both in and out of the water, creating moments and friendships that I will always treasure. It's hard to believe that it all came from the simple act of carrying a surfboard to the water's edge one September day long ago.

As for the unavoidable East Coast perspective throughout the pages of *Surf Lessons*, I make no apologies. I'm proud to let my East Coast freak flag fly, as many of these stories were rejected specifically because they were written from an East Coast point of view. Yes, our surfing experience is different in the East, and we have our own viewpoint and attitudes. But the bottom line is, and always was – we're still surfers, just like surfers anywhere else on the globe.

So, this is to all of us who: cut our teeth on fickle beach breaks; wait for the offshores on the backside of frontal systems; despise summer surf beaches and the crowds that come with them; know which one is the Garden State; bought a six-pack at a Brew-Thru during the never-ending drive to Hatteras; use a plastic shopping bag to thread our feet through a hooded 5/4 (Wawa is preferred in my area); can instantly name our all-time favorite hurricane swell.

I hope you enjoy and find some welcoming sandbars in *Surf Lessons*.

Earl Shores
August 2016

THE BEACH

Just over a year old and I'm on the beach in Ocean City, Maryland.
I'd already been there as a six-week-old, so it wasn't my first
experience. But I think it was my first beach experience where I
was cognizant enough to grasp that I was someplace special,
someplace I wanted to be, someplace that I liked a lot. Without the
additional thought or clutter that my brain would pick up by my
second birthday, I absorbed this beach experience like a sponge,
every cell in my body firing in a perfect sequence.

From my first steps on the sand, to my first toe in the ocean,
to the sunshine that warmed me like no other sunshine…I didn't
yet understand exactly what the beach was. But I did "get" the
general concept. Warm, fun – a giant sandbox with cool, rolling
water on the edge of it.

My parents fill out the background, so young, and probably
scared out of their minds over what the future held. They hadn't

been married all that long before I was born, and money was tight. Heck, we weren't even staying in Ocean City; we were staying across the bridge in a hotel along the barely developed Route 50 corridor.

In fairness, 1961 was a time when traffic in Ocean City wasn't all that challenging. By staying just across the bridge we were probably closer to downtown than if we stayed "up the beach" in one of the newly built motels along the boardwalk. Parking wasn't much of an issue either. And my family did know the place well. It's hard to believe, but at this point I was already the 4th generation of my family to put their toes in the Ocean City sand.

So there I am on the beach without a care in the world. Just wandering around the sand, mugging for the camera, soaking up the sun – life wasn't any better than that moment. Somehow I absorbed it all, all the sensations, all the pleasurable feelings, the total uncluttered Id of a very young child. It was the pure joy that you can only feel before you're aware of how scary and uncertain the world can be.

Somehow I soaked it all in…and fortunately, for the most part, it's still in there. I can still touch it. Not by some magic trance, or some forced reach into the past. All it takes are a few good waves, a few warm rays, a few moments hanging out on the sand, and life is as good as it was as a one-year-old. Maybe better, or sweeter, because of all that you go through while navigating five decades on this planet.

The beach is my place, my special place, and always will be. And it's something I've known, deep in my being, for nearly my entire life.

SUMMER SCHOOL

I stood alone by the 45th Street lifeguard stand, trying to convince my shaking hands to zip up my wetsuit jacket. The morning calm was broken by roaring walls of whitewater that seemed to glow against the ominous gray shades of the sea and sky. I hesitate now to estimate the size of the swell, but it was setting up as a "landmark" morning – and I hoped that five weeks of surfing experience had prepared me for it. Part of my nervousness came from the fact that none of my crew had shown up yet. This crew consisted of three other summer-transplant-beginners, and Andy, a local from work who adopted us and became our mentor.

My eyes surveyed the empty lineup, but kept wandering for frequent looks back across the vacant beach. Another surfer showed up and went out, pushing my heart rate into aerobic territory as my wax molded to my fingers. This couldn't be – of all the days where were they?

I made a decision to go solo and was surprised at how easily I got out. But while bobbing in stomach-losing peaks and horizon-less troughs, I realized that the takeoff would be my limiting factor.

It would have been easier with a little friendly peer pressure – someone to do it first and show me I wasn't going to die. But without my buddies, I floated aimlessly in a strange emotional cocktail of machismo and terror. I blew a fuse before finding my courage and scrambled like a wind up toy for the next wave I saw. As I got to my feet the board shot out from under my fear-stiffened body, and I skidded down the face in slow motion agony. In a panic, I struggled for the surface during the entire wash-cycle. (I *was* going to die!) After a comforting bounce off the sandy bottom, I surfaced for a breath that was met by the next wave of the set. Shaken and now out of breath, I paddled back out for a long rest.

I didn't die, but now that the consequences were no longer abstract, I wasn't ready for a second takeoff. Besides, nobody would ever know what happened. So what if I wimped out – nobody else even showed up.

My decision was almost made when Andy suddenly emerged from the back of a wave ten yards behind me.

"Some morning. How're you doing?" he asked. I shrugged. He smiled. "You're supposed to be having fun."

"Yeah, well let me know when it starts," I replied.

He was still smiling as he lifted himself off his board a bit and stretched for a better look at an incoming set. I relaxed – a little. I was glad that Andy had made it, and not someone who would be just as threatened by the conditions as I was. He quickly caught a wave, disappearing with a hoot behind the peak. He returned to my side with a wicked grin.

"Get ready," he said.

"For what?" I asked.

"We're gonna pick you out a wave. Have you taken off yet?"

"Yeah, but I fell off the back of the board. I'm not…"

"You're ready. You can handle it. Just be ready for the speed. It's not going to close out on you. You can do it, man, no sweat."

It was impossible to measure the importance of Andy's confidence. He was our surf guru – the first and last word in our new religion. If he thought I was ready, then maybe I was.

"Are you ready?" he asked, looking me dead in the eye. I forced a smile and shook my head up and down. The next set appeared much too soon. "Here we go, the second one, the second one!" Andy directed. I turned my board and began to paddle for the wave, my wavering inner voice focused by Andy's encouragement.

"Paddle, paddle, paddle! You got it, you got it!"

The wave picked me up and started to push me forward. I snapped to my feet, applied slight pressure with my front foot, and got ready for the drop. I knew I was going to make it. Andy's hoot faded as my momentum carried me to the bottom of the most exquisite roller coaster I'd ever ridden. I careened across the surging wave face just on the edge of control, finally finding a shoulder to kick out on. And that was it. In a blip it was over — but the buzz lingered. My mind's eye reran old Wide World of Sports footage of Waimea Bay, and I figured that was how I looked. (Well, that was how it felt.)

On my way back to the lineup I watched Andy gracefully maneuver to places that I never even noticed in my hurry to make the wave. For him it was a fun day, and he flowed easily with the power of the swell. To use his favorite term, he had it "wired." When he finally made it back to the lineup, we sat grinning at each other like two Cheshire cats.

"See? It was nothin'. You've got it wired now," he said.

"Well, almost nothing. It's still – "

"Aw, c'mon, man, you loved it! You're so stoked you could shit."

He was right.

A few waves later, when I was starting to feel comfortable, Andy asked for the time and called his last wave. How could he leave now? Ah, the early shift. I'd completely forgotten. As he waved from the beach I wondered if his abbreviated session had been worthwhile, but I was grateful he had come. I caught a final wave and came in. I hadn't been that excited about surfing since the first day I stood up.

That night at work I recounted the morning in understated terms to my truant surf buddies. They had overslept, or didn't think the cloudy morning held much promise for surf. Andy came over and started right in.

"Where the hell were you guys?" One of them started to explain but was cut off by Andy.

"The best day of the summer, and you missed it. Earl was there, and you shoulda seen him." After a brief pause for effect, Andy continued to lay it on thick. "He was jammin', man, like he'd been surfin' for years. I'd almost say he's a surfer. You guys gotta wait for the next big day to prove yourselves."

Everybody was quiet. Andy looked me in the eye, smiled, and walked away. I stood there flushed with embarrassment, but as he walked away I understood that his morning had been worthwhile. He was a very good teacher, and that summer we were his fortunate students. Imagine, me a surfer. Thirteen years later. I'm still amazed.

* *Summer School was accepted by Surfer magazine in the summer of 1992, but never published*

THE CHEAP THRILL SEEKERS

The sun was high overhead, sweat was running down my back – and I was beginning to have my doubts.

"Jesus Christ, John, get your shit in the boat," snapped Harry.

"Well, why don't you get the damn cooler yourself," John shot back. Tempers were running as hot as the weather, and I was trying to stay out of this. We were behind schedule, and the entire venture would collapse if we didn't get going soon. For Harry, or "Captain Harry" at this point, the cooler was just the latest point of contention.

"I ask you to get beer, and you show up with Old Milwaukee. That ain't beer, that's-"

"Slide the cooler over here," I said as I edged near the gunwale to help John lift the cooler. The boat was an eighteen-footer, but with three surfboards, a cooler, and three surfers, it was a little cramped. Harry fired up the engine…but it sputtered out.

"Great boat, Harry," said John. "Have a beer."

Harry flashed his lightning quick middle finger, and cranked the engine over again. This time she caught, and we pulled slowly away from the dock.

Out on the open water the breeze cooled down our bodies and our psyches. Like most surf trips the arrangements had been totally last minute, so everyone was wound a little tight. A few minutes wasted here, a few wasted there, the tide drops a little, the wind shifts ever so slightly – and you've got slop. Harry was at least partially right. If we blew this opportunity, Old Milwaukee would be little consolation.

We knew where we were going – sort of. That is, we knew where the waves were supposed to be, but we were sketchy on some of the minor details. Like, where to anchor the boat, what to do with the boards…or that industrial strength insect repellent was probably a good idea.

After twenty minutes we got to where we thought we should be and beached the boat on the backside of the island. The ocean seemed far away, but with my board under my left arm and a cooler handle in my right hand – John grabbed the other handle – we set off after Harry, who was already making his way toward the dune line.

At first it was faint. "Ouch! Dammit." Then a little louder. "OUCH!" We saw Harry's hand move quickly to the back of his neck. SLAP!! "Bastards!" Then to his leg. SLAP! Harry turned around. "Let's get the hell out of here!" he shouted, almost dropping his board as he bolted towards us.

"What's his problem?" said John. We hadn't quite figured it out yet, then I looked down at my legs. They were covered with brown specks – seems the blood bank was open in mosquito city.

"AAHHH!" I shouted, dropping the cooler while wiping both legs in a frantic sweeping motion. With a number of wounded with-drawlers still wriggling in my palm, I tried to pick up the cooler, but now John's end was on the ground. He was doing the mosquito-removal two-step too.

"Back to the boat, back to the boat!" I screamed. John picked up his end, and we now chased after Harry, who'd passed us while we discovered "his problem" for ourselves. Harry's board hit the bottom of the boat with a sickly thunk, and the boat rocked wildly as Harry jumped in like a salmon going up a waterfall.

"Start the boat!" shouted John, as he and I splashed into the shallows. The cooler went in with a thunk of its own, but I was more careful with my board than Harry was. "Start the boat!" shouted John again.

"I can't til we're in deeper water," Harry yelled back. John and I pulled the boat off the sandy bottom and pushed it toward the channel. It's a blur as to how we got back in, but Harry fired up the engine, which caught, fortunately, on the first try. With plenty of water under the propeller, we were safe.

"Damn," said Harry, admiring the welts on his arms. "Dirty little bastards." John started to laugh, and Harry gave him the stink-eye. "What? What's the matter with you?"

"It doesn't get any better than this," said John, laughing even harder after he uttered the all too well known Old Milwaukee catchphrase. I fell out laughing too, while Harry just sneered. "Pisswater," he said, "for a piss-poor time."

The welts were coming up nicely on my legs, merging into a mountain range of flesh. I tried my damndest not to scratch them, and broke the silence to distract my fingers.

"So now what?" I said.

"You tell me," said Harry.

"There must be a way to get to the waves."

"Yeah – how?"

"I don't know, let's just keep our eyes out."

"Yeah, I still want to get in the water," added John.

"Then why don't you jump over the side and swim home," said Harry.

John and Harry could go at it for hours, yet they shared a tent on surfaris. Go figure. Nothing personal, I guess. It was always great entertainment for those of us hanging around. Things could always go flat – but never quiet.

"We're not going out that damn inlet," said Harry, even though nobody had uttered a word about trying it. I sure as hell didn't want to try it either, but now that Captain Harry mentioned it, I worried that maybe he really did want to try it. All he needed was a dare. John and I weren't that stupid, and kept our mouths shut.

"Check out over there," said John, as we neared the mouth of the inlet. "Over there" was a sandy beach at the end of the island, which was protected by a long rock jetty. Another small boat was already anchored there – and empty. We pulled in closer, and saw the backspray of waves from just over the dune.

"This must be the place," I said. "Can we anchor?"

"I guess so," answered Harry. "Hope she doesn't drift out to sea."

John already had his board in his hand, and jumped over the side. "Hey!" shouted Harry. "You'll be paddling your ass home!" John just waved, paddled toward shore, and ran to the top of the dune. He waved us over, then disappeared as he descended down the other side.

"That little blond pecker. I oughta' fix his – "

"C'mon Harry, let's go," I interrupted.

"Shit, we should make him come back for the cooler."

We found John sitting at the water's edge watching head-high rights bowl up along the jetty.

"I was hoping you guys would get here soon," he said. "It's kind of smelly." He was right. Rotting clumps of seaweed and half-eaten crab carcasses littered the waterline, along with a dense band of wave-worn shells. Just a beach in its natural state – which isn't necessarily pretty.

One other surfer was out, and another was on the beach. There was not a mosquito to be seen. "I think we'll only have to watch out for these," said John, holding out his hand to display a giant green-headed horsefly. "They seem easy to catch."

And the waves were even easier – steep, fast, and consistent. A rotating lineup of four gave us ample opportunity to get the break wired. The jetty held the sand well, so the peak hardly shifted at all. The waves bowled up quickly, offering a little hollow section, but not much chance to maneuver. Especially backside. Just takeoff, grab the rail, and speed down the line. We got cocky, and started taking off deeper and deeper – only to get pounded harder and harder. Good thing the bottom was sand.

When the other surfers called it a day, the beach was totally empty. Looking to the South, there wasn't a soul as far as the eye could see. Just dunes, and backspray. To the North, you only saw the rocks of the jetty – that is, until the waves lifted you high enough to peek over this imposing, jagged gray wall. Then the sights and sound became even more exotic.

Our voyage had landed us on the North beach of Assateague Island – directly across the inlet from downtown Ocean City, Maryland. Just 500 yards away the Zipper was zipping, the Ferris wheel was turning, and the screams of fearful Wild Mouse riders filled the air as more than a quarter of a million tourists tried to live it up on a sweltering July afternoon.

So was our trip just a cheap thrill on a lazy summer day? Maybe. But at least we didn't cheapen it by opening the cooler.

* Originally published in Eastern Surf Magazine.

UNLIKELY SURF HERO

I stepped out of the car, two hours from the nearest ocean, decked out like a model from a *Surfer* magazine ad. Sky blue Lightning Bolt polo shirt, navy blue O.P. shorts, and leather Rainbow sandals on my feet. But I was totally cool. Inland department stores were still years away from marketing Surf City to the masses, so my clothes still had meaning. You couldn't buy them just anywhere. I didn't have them when I left home several months earlier, but my appearance wasn't the only thing that had changed since then.

After a decade of being a "dweebus wannabeus," I finally did it. I moved to the beach and learned to surf. It wasn't what I expected, though. I wanted to be a surf hero – you know, a cool dude trolling the crowded beaches with my surfboard, impressing all the tanned, young seasonal females. The Beach Boys scene and all that. But the waitresses at the seafood restaurant where I worked couldn't have cared less if you surfed. Your status in the restaurant caste system mattered most, and if you weren't a hunky smiling bus boy, you were essentially an untouchable.

My beach scene dreams were a bust too, because summer waves were usually the best early in the morning – when the beaches were empty. The funny thing was, it didn't matter. From my very first ride I understood that surfing had nothing to do with those things (well, maybe a little). Surfing was way beyond cool – and I knew my life would never be the same.

Still, the surf hero thing was an itch I wanted to scratch. I couldn't pull it off at the beach, but at home…that was a different story. By the time I graduated high school I was very much finished with my town. I had lived there my entire life, and after 18 years, the walls had closed in. It was somewhere I needed to leave, and in my head, I was determined never to return (another reason for living at the beach during the summer). But since morphing into a surfer, the new me felt ready for a visit.

Besides the surfer wardrobe, the new me included bushy sun-bleached hair, a deep tan, and after two months of surfing and carrying thirty-gallon crab-filled steam barrels around the restaurant, more shoulder and bicep girth than my body had ever seen. So I was ready to be "seen," showing off that I'd blown these boring streets and gone on to create an exotic life elsewhere.

Many of my old high school classmates were home from college, eking out a pedestrian summertime existence working fast food, or for dad, or whomever. And certain people I went out of the way to see as they cut lunchmeat or handed out prescriptions in the pharmacy. Cocky yet cool, I made sure to mention my beach existence without a torrent of Spicoli-syndrome vocabulary.

The person I was looking forward to seeing most was my old girlfriend. We hadn't seen each other in a year, hadn't been out with each other for almost two, but had been exchanging letters throughout the spring and summer. Her long-distance relationship with her boyfriend was on the rocks – well, actually it was over as far as she was concerned. The boyfriend, who had been her final high school boyfriend (succeeding me after my relationship with her fell apart), didn't quite understand that things were over, so she appreciated having someone male to share her frustrations with. I just wanted to be friends again…or at least that's what I kept telling myself.

A visit was arranged at her suggestion. I tried not to have great expectations, even though I had just worked 13 days in a row to get time off for the trip home. (The restaurant magnanimously gave me the final day off of one workweek, and the first day off of the next.) But it was hard not to feel excited as my Rainbows flapped over the stone path toward her house. I knocked on the door, standing tall, chest puffed out, the logos of my carefully chosen clothes announcing my wave brotherhood membership.

Her mother answered. A short pleasant woman who always made me feel comfortable, she remarked how good I looked as she led me to the rec room. She loudly announced my presence, and my heart sped up to a familiar "caught inside" rhythm. She stopped at the doorway and the moment was mine.

I knew I looked good. How could Corrine not swoon over the surf hero returning for the heart he so stupidly discarded two long years ago? It was better than I dreamed. I turned the corner to enter the room and our eyes met – mine and Thad's.

Talk about a "sneaker set."

Our eyes locked, and we eyed each other like territorial wolves…which I guess we were. Having faced a tropical storm groundswell just a week before, I had no reason to flinch, but when he finished with me, his eyes went to the floor and his body sunk deeper into the couch. He was the pale, slightly built, academic-type to begin with, and now he looked even worse.

I finally looked over at Corrine, who was on the couch with Thad, albeit a safe distance away. Her usually engaging brown eyes now had a pained in-the-headlights look. I wasn't sure what I walked in on, but I knew the situation was sticky.

Corrine and I carried the conversation during the 45 minutes I stayed. Benign stuff with lots of suffocating silences, it was a level of awkward that I'd never experienced. When Thad did join the conversation he didn't totally look at me, and his words stumbled out in faltering phrases. I was surprised. He had been one of the leads in the senior play, but that experience seemed to desert him now. I expected anger in his words, or at least an edge of contempt, but there was nothing. He just seemed numb.

Which is exactly how Corrine's letter explained it a few days later. I don't know how many sorry's she wrote, but apparently Thad showed up unannounced. She told him I was coming over, and he said he didn't mind. But when he saw me, he "froze" – those were her exact words.

So Thad had gotten his first look at a real live surf hero. I put down the letter and walked to the mirror – I wanted mine.

BIRD'S EYE

The low sun blinds me through a slowly defrosting windshield, so the color of the traffic light twisting in the stiff offshore is still a mystery. It figures. Hell, there are only half a dozen red lights in town still working, and I've hit two. But I don't dare go through it. There's probably a cop nearby, jumbo java in hand and a bag from Donut Junction, trying to scrape up the monthly quota. Since the Range Rover and Beamer crowds took their Amstel-Light swilling asses home months ago, the steady red-light running income dried up. Now the cops pick on the locals. I'd probably get written up for obstructed view, or some other stupid shit – so I sit.

My left hand shields the sun, while my right hand probes behind the seat for a napkin or paper towel. Pennies, sand, and rocks of wax are all my numbed fingers find before the light changes. At least I think it changed – but I have margin for error. The car sputters and coughs in cold-carburetor distress before lurching forward with three head-snapping jerks.

Defroster hiss overpowers cheap-speaker reggae distortion, but not even 500 bass-tube booming watts of Bob Marley could convince me it was summer. Each frosty exhale clues me in, along with my board chattering against the rack like a frozen Sugar Daddy. I've got one more stop, and I'm hoping to find just one thing.

Somebody out.

Blustery Northwest winds have knocked down the swell since midnight, but wind-scoured grinders still peel righteously this morning. I've made several phone calls just after sunrise, and the explanations for them going unanswered could be work, women, hangovers, or balls – I'm not one to pass judgment. Still the question – Alex, I'll take wind-chill factor for a $1000 – why is nobody out?

I make a turn, but only one rack-less car inhabits the street. The sun's glare pierces my eyes, and it takes a moment to focus on the lineup. Yeah, I knew it – empty. The last three waves of a five wave set look really sweet as they feather and backspray in the wind. My eyes draw lines beyond my ability, inspired by corporate-sponsored-pro-surfer-South-Pacific-video fantasies. Shit, this ain't G-Land – it's Maryland. In January no less. A lip bash becomes more of a lip mash when you're covered in more rubber than the *Creature from the Black Lagoon*.

I hang out, still drawing imaginary lines on the sets. Wind gusts rock the car and the cassette finishes, flipping over to the other side. Midnight Oil, painting Australian audio landscapes…with more distortion than they intended. Yeah, maybe someday I'll get a new stereo – and maybe someday I'll get to Australia. Like the day after I win the lottery. Then I could stop worrying about these little things like food and rent.

I take off my shoes, crank the heat, and stuff my feet up into the vent. Ah, warmth. I'd crank the stereo, but it's pointless. I'm here, alone, and it's decision time. The word "alone" doesn't go well with cold, for me anyway. But I'm here. Alone. So what? Hardcore, that's me. Mr. Hardcore. Fuckin'a, man let's do it.

What's the worst that can happen? The wind blows me to France? Hell, that's what the Coast Guard is for. Do it, man, do it!

The car is too small, so my sweatpants are off when I open the door and drop a towel on the frigid asphalt. I do the damp-wetsuit two-step, letting the car shelter me from the wind, and with a ballet of trained reflexes, fling my sweatshirt into the car, scramble my arms down the sleeves, and pull my head into the attached hood. Leaning back ever so slightly I grab the zipper with my left hand and yank it from right to left across my shoulders. *Ziiiip.* Goose bump city. I stuff my feet up in the vent one last time, put on my boots and wrestle with my lobster claw, hoping my incisors don't rip the sleeve of my suit.

Mini sandstorms blow across the beach, and my boots aren't thick enough to ward off the sand's chill. Lines on my face get deeper squinting out to the horizon, where wispy lines of clouds hover in a limitless blue, and merge with the offshore whitecaps. Near the water a small group of sea gulls face the wind, shuddering as their feathers get blown smooth by the gusts. One lets out a distinctive call, arches out his wings, and flaps gently to rise upward and away from the others.

Yep. Sometimes you just gotta' go it alone.

* Originally published in Eastern Surf Magazine.

A QUITTER'S STORY

A comforting coffee burp blew past the toothpick clenched between my teeth, leaving the tangy hickory vapor of bacon on the back of my palate. Breakfast is taken seriously in the South, and the cholesterol-killer-over-easy-lard-biscuit-gut-buster we ingested at Cap'n Daves left us waddling to the car like four fat cats looking for someplace to lick their bellies. But there was reason for celebration and indulgence – well, overindulgence if you want to get particular. We had just scored early-morning overhead Lighthouse, surfing ourselves silly before the crowds arrived. And now, with our fill of waves and calories, we set off to find a relaxing way to kill a beautiful August day on the Outer Banks.

The price of the morning – our jobs – was kind of steep, but the summer only had two weeks left and we had made enough money. What we wanted was time, but the supervisors at our place of employment – an Ocean City, Maryland slave galley masquerading as a seafood restaurant – decided they couldn't afford to let us all have several days off. Their "bottom line" stance was lost on a surfing foursome two weeks overdue for a promised 10 cent raise, so we rewarded ourselves with a deep-fryer mutiny at 5 o'clock on Saturday night. Exiting the restaurant like giggling school children headed for recess, we parted a line of customers that wound halfway around the block, knowing their wait had just gotten a little bit longer.

The unity of our uprising was remarkable, considering that when the summer began, we didn't know each other – or how to surf. And without surfing, we would have never hung out together. There was Harry, the spoiled smart-ass Washington, D.C. suburbanite; John, the handsome Baltimore prep school jock; Jack, the small town good ol' boy; and me, the lifetime wannabe who earlier in the summer would have sold his soul for someone to surf with. But the unforeseen power of surfing rearranged our lives, and we became like one of those "cross section of America" platoons from a cheesy B war movie – best buddies. Better yet, hard-core surfing buddies, and nothing else mattered.

The daily lessons we received from a benevolent local (our kitchen crew chief) quickly removed us from kookdom, and smoothed our paths into the universe of surfing. He also supplied fuel for our revolt with tales of almond-shaped barrels, powerful lefts, and empty lineups at the Eastern wave-magnet, Cape Hatteras. By August, our transformation into the exotic life form known as a surfer needed one more step – a surfari, and Hatteras was the logical choice. After rounding up some camping gear, we headed south Monday morning in a vehicle Jack borrowed from the "take good care of the car, son" agency. The deal, unlimited mileage and just pay for fuel, was too good to pass up, even though the potential consequences were severe (lifetime guilt). Our evening arrival delivered us into some slightly onshore but fun surf at the Lighthouse, giving us a chance to indulge in rides that seemed three times as long as we were used to. That session on its own made the trip worthwhile, but the morning surpassed all of our expectations.

With our youthful cast-iron stomachs providing no-drama digestion, we piled into the car stoked for a commemorative T-shirt search. The Fox Surf Shop was our chosen destination, but along with T-shirt designs, board prices became the major topic of conversation. At least with Harry. He was still riding a loaner, and was now frothing at new boards priced $100 less than at Ocean City surf shops. He didn't have enough cash on the trip for such an investment, so the rest of us offered a combined loan – which made Harry circle the boards like a feeding shark. Unfortunately, the array of "prey" overwhelmed him, and he couldn't make a decision before we left to check out the dying swell.

The Lighthouse was ruled out because of the crowds, so I was given scouting duties when we stopped at the One Way Road – probably because I was riding shotgun. The sand burned my feet as I hurried through a clearing in the sea oats, and a hot west wind blew the hood of my sweatshirt against the back of my head when I reached the top of the dune. Empty swells fought hard against the offshore wind to become something other than shorebreak, but few had success, and I could see that two other surfers had already resigned themselves to catching rays on the beach. I moved quickly back down the sunbaked sand.

"Might be rideable – it's worth a try," I reported.

"Whadaya mean, MIGHT be," mocked Harry, "Is it or isn't it?"

"Come look for yourself."

The four of us made double-time up the dune, and it looked like the swell had given up.

"I'll go out," volunteered John, peering out from under the brim of his Bronzed Aussie hat – which matched his Cheyne Horan model surfboard. "I'd rather be in the water than in the car."

"Yeah, hell, why not. Ain't much summer left," said Jack.

Harry also made a decision: "I wanna go back and get a board."

"Oh, so now that it's flat you'll take our money?" I deadpanned.

"Yeah, maybe we changed our minds," said John.

Harry stood silently, but I couldn't keep a straight face any longer. John and Jack broke up laughing too.

"Assholes. Gimme the money," said Harry.

"How you gettin' back there?" said Jack, giving an uncharacteristic late hit.

"Huh? Gimme the keys then. I'll drive myself," said Harry, as he started toward the car.

"You think I'm gonna let you drive my car?" continued Jack, while the laughter from John and me escalated.

Harry offered us a finger, and the three of us followed him to the car, where he leaned against the white vinyl roof, smirking at us for a moment before his mischievous smile beamed from a three month "no sunscreen" tan.

"C'mon guys, I want a board."

We knew – but Harry deserved a little harassment. He spent the summer dishing it out, especially to John, who was still too naïve to understand he was a preppie. This innocence made John all the more likeable, and sometimes Jack and I headed off Harry when his needle got a little too sharp. But most times, Harry found deserving targets for his caustic comments…including himself.

"Git in, I'll take you," offered Jack, selfless as always, "but I wanna hurry and get back before it gets flat." Shading his thick glasses with a thick hand, he squinted an exaggerated smile at Harry.

"So everybody's a comedian today, huh?" said Harry. Jack wasn't very often, but we savored the moments he was.

Harry got our extra money, and he and Jack both chortled, "Save us some waves" as the car pulled away. John and I hotfooted it over the dune and toward the water.

"That was a great ride this morning – the one where you almost ran over Harry," chuckled John, stripping the T-shirt from a chiseled physique that generated dreamy-eyed gazes from the waitresses all summer long.

"Yeah, I was lucky to get that wave to myself. The crowd was getting heavy," I said, once again feeling like the skinny sand-in-the-face "before" kid in those comic book weightlifting ads.

"We won't have to worry about that here."

"Nah, and those guys seem dead to the world," I said, nodding toward the two sunbathing surfers down the beach.

The warm water felt cool after a few minutes on the beach, and we paddled leisurely toward a smooth horizon defined by various blue shadings from a Crayola 64 box. As large puffy clouds drifted lazily overhead, deciding where the lineup was, if there was one, appeared to be our most difficult task. We were still paddling gently when the horizon suddenly sat up. I looked over at John.

"Do you see that?" I said.

"Think so – can't be, though," he answered.

We kept moving, picking up the pace a little while arching up on our boards for a better view.

"Shit, I don't believe it. Outside!" I shouted.

"Wooaah…let's go!" added John.

The race was on. A building set of five waves closed in as our unprepared nervous systems shifted from third to overdrive – and our reactions sputtered accordingly. Maybe it was the extra weight from breakfast, but number five was faster than me, and the lip of a top-to-bottom wave, the likes of which I'd never faced before, exploded on my back. The board was gone in flash, and after the initial take down, it had enough power to suck me back over-the-falls. When I finally surfaced, my board floated in the foamy remnants of the wave, pointing out toward the once again smooth horizon. John was nearby, struggling to mount his board through a fit of coughs. I caught his eye, and my smile quickly turned to a laugh.

"Where the hell did they come from?" he asked, now laughing too.

"I don't know, but I hope they keep coming," I said.

They did.

For the next 45 minutes John and I were in goofy-footer heaven, taking off on one overhead almond-shaped left after another. Each wave seemed the same – steep drop, make a quick turn, look down the line to infinity, and scream yourself hoarse while racing the pitching lip to the shoulder. The tube became a reality for both of us, and through burning arms and heaving chests, we continued chasing waves that never closed out. The sets got sporadic, and our arms stopped listening to our brains, but the tongue wagging smiles on our faces said it all.

Finally, Harry marched over the dune like a hunter with his conquest, triumphantly holding up his new possession for us to see. Four arms frantically motioned him and Jack to the lineup, though no sets came through as they paddled out.

"Where in the hell have you been?" said John. "You missed it."

Harry thought his abuse from the morning was continuing.

"Yeah, sure we missed it. What, you guys pickin' your noses?"

"No, man, you *really* missed. It's been great. Really." I said, "Just you wait."

Jack sensed that I wasn't kidding around. "You ain't shittin' us, are you?"

I just shook my head back and forth.

Some occasionally impressive sets rolled through, not as good as earlier, but good enough to back up the seemingly incredulous story that John and I couldn't stop telling. We hated to pop Harry's new board bubble of excitement, but there was no way around it – they had missed it.

By Thursday it was flat, and we dropped John off in Nags Head where his brother had been living for the summer. That was the last time I saw him – and that was 1979. But the image of the four of us basking in the shadow of the Lighthouse has come to mean one thing. The surf trip of a lifetime.

Thanks guys.

---

* A Quitter's Story was rejected by Surfer and The Surfer's Journal, finally getting published on Surfline.com. It also won a custom longboard in an East Coast writing contest sponsored by the Global Surf Network.

TRICK OR TREAT

The phone outside my dorm room rang, then came a knock on the door. It was for me. I sat up in the darkness, my heart kicking in the nervous rhythm of sudden arousal. Maybe my recently evasive girlfriend in Boston came to her senses?

"Hello?"

"Hey dude, what's up?" It was only Harry, my surfing buddy from Salisbury State. "I just bought a tent."

"Yeah, so?"

"Come on, man, let's go. Fuckin' full moon – Halloween in Hatteras. It's perfect."

"Shit Harry, I got class – and a test next week." This answer was pure reflex. He knew I didn't need much coaxing.

"Wuss," said Harry, invoking the lowest of surfing life forms, the surfari "wuss."

"Are there any waves in O.C.?"

"Who needs waves in O.C.? We're fuckin' talkin' about Hatteras, man."

"Alright, alright. I'll pick you up tomorrow afternoon."

Stupid-ass hunches were common in the pre-900-SURF and Weather Channel days, and sometimes the stupider the hunch, the better. (Soul Surfing at its finest.) So as a sunset glow fell on the rustic dilapidation of Virginia's lower Eastern Shore, we tooled down Route 13 through the crisp fall air, trading swigs on a bottle of Old Setter. By the time we reached the label, my growing internal glow saw Halloween in Hatteras for what it was – a "killer" idea.

The eerie lighted expanse of the Chesapeake Bay-Bridge Tunnel provided stoke (the first water we saw on the trip), and exiting I-64 at Route 158 deposited us into the southernmost reaches of Tidewater civilization. An abandoned dumpster offered cover for a wicked whiskey wiz, and we stocked up at a last chance 7-11 for our run through rural eastern Carolina – two bags of Cheetos and a six-pack of Busch beer.

We fired up the car, fired up a joint, and savored "the cheese that goes crunch" as the empty two-lane-tree-lined highway to Hatteras became the "Highway To Hell" with the help of AC/DC.

Shortly after midnight we pulled up to the Lighthouse, and as its interval flashed over the water we tried to make out the size of the swell. We couldn't get a good look, but the roaring whitewater seemed to be a good sign. Since the National Park campground office was closed at this hour of the night, we retreated to one of the oceanside motels in Buxton where a buzzer-awakened owner suspiciously eyed two slightly buzzed and road weary surfer types. He agreed to rent us a room only if we left the boards on the car.

Sure dude, whatever you say. *Yeah, right.*

Sometime before the sun came up, the fishermen in the units around us decided to warm up their trucks – unmuffled, over-sized, V-8, four-wheel drive, Detroit rustbucket shit. Vibrations rattled the room, and this airport decibel din was accented by cacklin' good ol' boy chatter. I pulled the pillow over my head and prayed to whatever god was listening for just another hour of sleep.

They left – eventually – and I finally roused from my musty synthetic blanket to throw on some clothes. It was chilly, but the wind was light offshore. So what if I only had a spring suit, the water would keep my legs warm. Near the ocean, though, it was quiet, and as I walked over the dune I couldn't believe what my puffy eyes saw. Fishermen. And not just a few, it looked like the whole damn state of North Carolina had taken the day off. I mean, that's what it sounded like earlier, but hell, who expected this? Lined up as far as I could see, to the north and to the south, were beach buggies and fishermen…and fishermen, and more fishermen. There wasn't even a break in the line to get to the ocean.

And the ocean – AAARRRRGGHH! Flat. Dead flat, with just a few dumpy peaks of shorebreak every now and then. I closed my eyes slowly and opened them again. No change. I got in the car and hustled off to the Frisco Pier – same conditions. We were screwed.

"It's flat, Harry," I said when I returned.

"Huh?"

"It's flat. With a capital 'F.' And there's fishermen everywhere. Fuckin' flat with fishermen!"

"Maybe the Southside–"

"I was there, same thing."

"Maybe tomorrow– "

"Let's just get the hell out of here. It's just too weird."

"Wuss."

The picture I took of Harry flashing me the finger from a swell-less Lighthouse lineup pretty much said it all. After enduring dinner at Crickets with a half-dozen fatigue clad fishermen staring down the longhairs (us), we froze our asses off in the tent, having only the blankets that Harry "borrowed" from the motel. Finally, I wasted our dinnertime fortitude by spewing cheesesteak sub in the middle of the night (just in case I didn't realize how stupid it was to order a cheesesteak in North Carolina).

The drive home the next day was long – and silent.

Fuckin' full moon Halloween in Hatteras – yeah, killer.

* Originally published in Eastern Surf Magazine.

BEAR OF THE BANKS

This time I was ready. Ready to erase the humiliation of the previous year, when my new girlfriend and I ventured to the Outer Banks of North Carolina for a wretched but memorable experience. Thanks to the full bloom of youthful stupidity, I let my surf skills wither during a semester of inland collegiate hibernation. Yet as a surf-stud-in-progress, I still thought I could handle the frigid March Atlantic and show off my surfing "lifestyle." In between watching the locals jump into the lineup from a fishing pier, and abandoning our tent for a lack of bilge pumps, I managed to paddle out on three consecutive days and not catch a wave. By the time I made it to the lineup my lifeless arms flailed about my body as if the sleeves of my wetsuit were empty. With no hope of catching a wave, I proned in on the first set that rolled through. (My explanation to my girlfriend: "Sometimes surfing is like that.")

But this year was different. Amazingly, after that fiasco, my girlfriend remained my girlfriend and we were now living together.

With a new tent, a new stove, an air mattress, reservations at a sheltered campground, and months of lap swimming under my belt, I felt prepared. So after a late evening arrival and a peaceful night's sleep, we watched an empty chest-high Lighthouse swell shimmer in the mid-morning sun.

Three other surfers were paddling out, but I lost sight of them when I got to the water's edge. Encased in stiff rubber from head-to-toe, my mind focused on my arms. What was going to happen this year? I had to be in better shape than last year, right? Sure, just get in the water. I'll be fine.

I felt pretty good as I made my way through the shorebreak, and over the deep hole where the waves re-formed. And when I reached the initial part of the sandbar where the dissipating whitewater rolled in, I still felt okay. I slowed down, waiting for a lull, and when it came, I ordered my neoprene-laden arms to move as fast as they could. My progress was steady, and the feedback from my arms encouraging, but when another set started forming outside it was obvious that I underestimated the size of the swell – by about half.

I scratched over the first wave (come on arms, come on), but as I pushed under the second one, my body wasn't quite ready for one small detail.

The 40°F water.

The most troubling part of the shock wave that assaulted my spinal column was the involuntary decision by my lungs to expel their air. The momentary paralysis of all my limbs seemed trivial by comparison. In backyard football terms I had the wind knocked out of me, but at the moment it wasn't possible to lie on the ground and get my breath back. I emerged from the back of the wave, still on my board, gasping and wheezing in oxygen-debt agony while another frosty wall closed in. With my body too far gone to go any further, the only effect of this wave was to knock me off my board. I surfaced with my condition unchanged – uncomfortably numb.

I drifted in the lull, trying to coax coherence out of my

anesthetized gray matter, but when the next set came, I was still unable to offer any resistance and got pushed into the re-form section. Although my arms didn't really feel that bad, my head and heart were frozen. So I came in to thaw out on the beach, letting my artificial black skin soak up the sun's warmth like some kind of mutant seal.

When my core body temperature clambered out of hypothermia range, my tremors subsided and I noticed two waterlogged figures just down the beach sharing my listless state. There was some consolation in outlasting them, but we were truly a pathetic bunch who watched with thawing envy as a lone silhouette caught a significant set wave and came in.

I was disappointed, but not crushed like the year before. My girlfriend had actually seen me surf in the interceding year, so that pressure was gone. We joked a little about the encore performance, and were just content to be on the beach enjoying the sunshine. As we watched the unridden sets, something moved into the far right side of my vision. With a slight turn of the head I saw a burly figure approaching. My mouth went dry as he neared, for I assumed I was in for a first-hand lesson in localism. When he finally stopped, I looked up and realized that I underestimated size – again.

He stood well over six-feet tall, dark hair falling to his muscular shoulders, while a barrel chest challenged the limits of the wetsuit that clung tightly to his body. A bushy beard and a determined squint accented his dripping dishevelment, summoning visions of Blackbeard reincarnated. My ears went red, and began pulsing a cardiac code of distress.

"How y'all doin' today?" he said with a characteristic Carolina coastal draw, and a tone that was slightly higher and softer than my fear predicted. I don't know if my relief was audible, but my Northeastern cynicism wondered what his angle was. Key chain beach pictures maybe?

"I see you had a little trouble gittin' out," he continued, "I wanna' go back out, but these other guys – well, they said they're done for the day. I don't like surfin' by ma'self, so if you're up for it, I can git' you out."

My brain whirred and clicked on his offer. Was he for real? "Southern Hospitality" was only a term from trashy romance novels, right? Finally with a glow of a schoolboy who'd been picked to run the filmstrip projector, I said, "Sure."

"Great!" he said, and a wide patch of white parted the dark thicket under his nose. He held out his hand. "I'm Delbert – you know, like Delbert McClinton the singer," he said, referencing an artist who recently had a Billboard Top 10 single. Delbert still had a head on me when I stood up, and his hand swallowed mine in a modest grasp.

"My friends call me Bear."

I didn't have to ask why.

Reality seemed a little distant as we headed down toward the shorebreak, but when he stopped to reassure my girlfriend with model "southern gentleman" gentility – "Don't worry ma'am, I'll take good care of him" – the chill reappeared in my wetsuit. I waited for a diabolical baritone narrator and eerie dissonant music.

"Presented for your approval, a young surfer who wanted nothing more than to catch a wave..."

"Where y'all from?" asked the Bear.

"Huh," I sputtered, startled back to reality.

"Where y'all from?" the Bear repeated patiently.

"Oh, uh, Delaware," I answered.

"Oh yeah? Sometimes we do work off a' there."

"Work?"

"Yeah, fishing mostly."

"Do you live around here?"

"A mile or so down the road."

"Nice."

"It's interesting, that's for sure."

The small talk ended at the waterline, where I listened closely to the Bear's instructions.

"We're going to head out on the south side of this jetty here. We can float in the rip without even paddling. Then at the end there's some deep water where we can sit til' we get a lull. It's easy today because the swell is small."

"Small?" I asked

He looked at my incredulous expression and re-evaluated.

"Well…I mean, it's a fun day for here. You understand what we're doin?"

I nodded, and we waded into the rip current, floating out effortlessly alongside the jetty just like the Bear said.

I kept looking over at my giant new companion, unsure if it was the rip or the Bear's aura that pulled me along. I seemed reduced to monosyllable responses in his presence. Not that I felt threatened in any way. The fact was, I felt oddly and totally secure next to the Bear, even though we'd only shaken hands five minutes earlier. My well-trained skepticism was about to tackle this conundrum, when the Bear looked over, held both hands out of the water, and let his giant smile once again cut the through the dripping brush on the bottom of his face.

"See, I'm keepin' right up with ya'," he said.

"Uh-huh," escaped my mouth before my brain found something intelligent to say. But my skepticism now retreated like a scolded puppy.

We reached the end of the jetty and paddled in place for a few moments as the Bear carefully watched the horizon. He then turned and grinned, "Let's go!!"

With long powerful strokes he quickly left me behind, and I felt like once again I was in over my head. I worked my arms furiously, and could hardly believe it when they responded. The Bear angled to the south, while I took the shortest route to the lineup, which was straight ahead. With not a set in sight it was a dry-hair paddle out. Was there ever a doubt?

I sat catching my breath, looking twenty yards south to where the Bear sat. I wanted to paddle down and thank him and learn more about surfing the Lighthouse, but I knew my energy was limited. So I waved and gave him a thumbs-up. He smiled, returning my wave, then fixed his gaze on the undulating horizon.

After two fun rides I came in to watch the Bear ride his home break. He toyed with several overhead waves, surfing with expected power, but also a surprising grace as he easily found the pocket on each wave. He really made it look easy.

I walked down to meet the Bear when he came in.

"Did you git' some waves?" he asked.

"Yeah, I got two. Thanks a lot, I woulda' never made it out today."

"Oh, you're welcome. Glad I could help. You come back after lunch and it'll probably still be good. Tides gonna' change – might even pick up some."

That was a daunting thought, especially since cold water fatigue was starting to settle deep into my muscle fibers.

"Yeah, we'll stop back up. See ya' then," I said, unsure if I was being completely truthful about my intentions.

"Okay, y'all take care now," the Bear replied.

My girlfriend and I did go back later, but the beach was completely empty. The wind had gone onshore, turning the previously glassy swell into a foaming crumbling mess, and I shivered easily as the chilly ocean air pierced my sweatshirt. It was hard to believe how pleasant it had been earlier, and even harder to believe the actual events of the morning. But I'll always be grateful for the friendly stoke and memorable session I shared with a gentle giant known as the Bear.

THE RITUAL

A car horn assaults my ears over the high-speed hum of the window fan. My eyes open and struggle to focus because the room is filled with the shadowy strobe effect of sunlight and fan blades. The giggles of tourists serve as a snooze button, and these people complete my unwilling quest for consciousness by slamming three car doors under my window. Ah summer, lovely summer.

The tourists come from Shangri-La – the motel next door – and several times this month we've had the pleasure of calling the police to chase their cars out of our backyard. This group is up early for a weekday, and on another morning I might have been thankful for their noise. But with this Bermuda High system hanging over us, they're just a pain in the ass.

As I sit up, I can tell that the cool of the morning isn't that cool. Even with the fan set on "max," the air seems reluctant to move, bringing out the beach smell of our Spartan seasonal rental. A week of three graveyard and two regular shifts has produced puffy eyes, and a grogginess that lingers no matter how much I sleep. The bed feels good, and I'm tempted to lie back down. But I have to get up.

The Ritual begins.

My roommate sleeps on a mattress on the floor. As usual, he's crashed out with his bartending clothes still on. I never heard him come in, and wonder if he remembered to lock the door. After lucking out and getting a job at this summer's new hot spot, he's been keeping an uncomfortably large sum of tip money under his mattress. While I subsist on scrapple and beans, he's buying cases of Foster's. But it's cool, he shares his wealth and helps me out when I need it.

I grab my lucky sweatshirt off the door knob, use a hat instead of a comb, and head out into the darkness of the long main hallway. My left hand grazes the wall to balance my unsteady shuffle, and measures my progress by feeling the simulated joints in the paneling. The kitchen-living area is darkened by tightly-drawn venetian blinds, but the light hanging over the kitchen table casts unflattering shadows that draw my eyes like a car accident.

Dirty pots on the counter emit a congealed grease aroma, patiently waiting their turn in a sink overrun by several meals' worth of debris. Blackened bananas offer breakfast to a genetics class worth of fruit flies, while empty beer cans in the nearby garbage can discharge a pungent yeasty chaser. Neatly stacked newspapers threw a party during the night, leaving numerous sections passed out all over the couch. And finally, a chair facing the television is surrounded by a sea of Cap'n Crunch that didn't quite make it into the mouth of my munched-out roommate.

I reach the door and step outside.

My eyes squint under sunglasses, even though the sun hides behind a ten-story beachfront condo building. The light offshore wind feels good, but my sweatshirt lives up to its name. This wind will blow harder as the sun rises higher, and feel like an oven blast by the afternoon. The weather radio made no predictions of frontal systems or tropical activity, so the depressing weather pattern of the last several days will continue.

The morning surf check was more fun before I started following the weather closely. I didn't realize that learning to anticipate those rare great days would also mean knowing about all the other flat days — and this is one more day when I hope that my proudly cultivated surf forecasting skills are wrong.

I step off the peeling stairs and survey the price of living on a beach block, as cars occupy every legal inch of it. Fifteen yards to the west Coastal Highway comes to life, but at the moment you can still cross it without a pair of starting blocks (although waiting for the evening gridlock might be the only way to make it back). Apart from the condo at the end, our street is lined with the assorted pastel shades of traditional two- and three-story summer only cottages. Their disjointed webs of white-trimmed steps and porches connect to the sidewalk like the work of an inebriated spider.

As I walk toward the ocean there is sporadic activity. Kids on a porch carefully check their toys, questioning through a window when they can go to the beach; an older couple sits out drinking coffee, reading a newspaper that has been carefully folded for the breeze; and the heavenly smell of frying bacon drifts from an undetermined origin. For the tourists, it's just another day in paradise on this quiet morning. But the usual bounce in my surf-check step is gone. It's just too quiet.

The last 10 yards of the street are slightly uphill, and I can gauge the size of the swell by where I am when I first see waves. Today, I run out of street. The ocean offers a pathetic little swell that doesn't even make the Sandpipers run. I'm disappointed, and disappointed that I'm disappointed. Hell, I knew it was flat since I opened my eyes.

It's still beautiful though. A hazy sun shimmers across the swell-less glassy expanse, and the beach is empty and smooth except for the tracks of the overnight cleanup trucks. The water has warmed recently, and it could have been a pleasant "trunks only" morning. For a brief moment I'm enticed by beauty, and hope and desperation have me considering putting my twin-fin on the car to cruise the town.

"Forget it, it's FLAT!" says rationality.

"Maybe the inlet is holding some peaks," answers desperation.

"Riiiiight. Did we surf yesterday?"

"Well no, but – "

"But we weren't as desperate yesterday? Come on, you're going to risk a parking place for this dribble? If there's one other idiot out, it'll be too crowded!"

"Won't it be worth losing a spot if we can surf?"

"Man, get a grip, these graveyards are making us crazy."

"What could it hurt…"

"Shut up already. Relax, get some coffee, read the paper, enjoy the morning. It's only July, man."

"I guess you're right. There's always tomorrow."

"It's one of the best things about surfing."

(Why does it have to be so hard?)

I watch the sun move a little higher, and head back to the apartment content that later, I'm not going to hear about some obscure no-swell-low-tide-sandbar in the state park being "all-time." The street is still quiet, unlike the days when I walk back after surfing and my roommate is up, serenading the neighbors with concert volume levels of "Planet Claire" while psyching himself up for a run. Today I keep walking past our still-drawn windows and head for the Royal Farms store across the highway. As I step into my starting blocks, I'm glad that I listened to rationality – but it's going to be a long, long day.

* Originally published in Eastern Surf Magazine.

THE DAY THE CALYPSO SANK

Although the summer was over, and my college sheepskin sat in a cardboard tube by the end of the bed, my "Reaganomics" reward was the four-to-midnight shift at the 84th Street Exxon. Yeah, I'd weaseled an oceanfront condo for the winter, complete with indoor swimming pool, but gas jockey wasn't my ultimate goal. In reality, I was Jacques Cousteau Jr. – only some graduate schools couldn't recognize that from my grades and GRE scores.

That was okay, I had a plan. I'd hang out, take a few courses, beef up my GPA, and study for my next crack at the GRE's during shifts at the station. I'd also get a little surfing in. You know, just for fun. Then next year I'd be in graduate school for sure.

September was a breeze and a blast. Spring suits became full suits, dawn patrols were delayed, and evening sessions ended earlier as the sun drifted back toward the equator. But the good swells and lack of crowds were more than an even trade. Hell, when it was flat, I did laps in the pool. Work was getting slower by the week, yet it wasn't as easy to study as I thought.

If only I could turn off the TV at the station.

My first human physiology exam was scheduled for early October, and I was hanging in, almost up on the readings, and eating up the lectures. The professor had a thoroughly nasty rep, but he wasn't getting me. It was probably the quarts of coffee I guzzled during the 90-minute drive to campus, but this class was important. Severely important. A "mission from God" you might say.

I was scheduled to work the 8-to-4 shift on exam day, so I planned the final study push for the day before. I was only a chapter behind on the readings and felt confident with the lectures. There was only one thing I didn't plan for – sunny and 80°F with offshores gently grooming chest high sets.

The day didn't start like that. A quick look out my oceanfront window before breakfast revealed only warm westerlies and a dribbling swell. A break from the books at 11 A.M., however, showed a dropping tide with building sets. My well-conditioned surfer instincts tried to kick in, but I caught them. I had to study. I couldn't mess around, this class was my future. So I went back to my books, but my mind was straying. Have some more coffee, yeah that's it – but it wasn't. Things got worse. Waves. All I could think about was waves. No, no, no, back to the books, actin, myosin, calcium channels, sodium pumps…ADRENALIN.

I settled for a lunchtime surf break, deciding to "trunk it" as a safety valve for a short session. A few waves, and I'd be done, especially with the water temp hovering around 60°F. I felt naked walking across the beach without a layer of rubber, crossing paths with a retired couple that happened to be panting along the sand in sweaters and long pants. They weren't the only ones surprised by the sun's warmth. But this high noon heat was going to be much needed when I hit the water.

Or so I thought.

Somehow I waltzed right into the shorebreak like it was August on the Outer Banks, or summer on the Space Coast. Was this really October in the mid-Atlantic? My body didn't even offer up a shiver when the water reached the Velcro of my Surf-Lites.

I caught a few fun waves and basked in this stunning climatic convergence. (Who'd a thought, you know?) There were even some hollow sections on the sets. I checked my watch. One o'clock – ok, just a few more sets. Oops, 2 o'clock. One more wave, just one more. The shadows of the high rises began creeping across the beach as the dropping tide brought more barrels than before. OH SHIT – 3:20! I had to get my ass to work. And the test. Shit!

I studied at work that night, and even some after work, but I felt an imaginary surf leash tightening around my neck. The next day counted down much too quickly as my brain tried to suck facts out of the final assigned chapter while divvying out Marlboro Lights and 10W-40. Before I knew it I was on the road, large coffee in hand, driving toward the sunset and my destiny.

It's usually nice to be one of the first people to finish an exam. On this particular evening, I just wanted to get a drop form to the Continuing Ed office before it closed. I never found out what I got on that test, and I never made it to graduate school – but I still surf. And when I'm out in the lineup on one of those rare yet glorious Indian summer days, I think back…and wouldn't change a damn thing.

* Originally published in Eastern Surf Magazine.

10/25/82

I wonder how many other people are thinking this might be _the_ swell, the one we wait a lifetime for. Are there other wondering what will happen when the wind finally turns offshore, cleaning up the raging froth the ocean has whipped itself into. Will we wake up one morning looking at 8 foot barrels peeling with the machine like precision we only see in magazines. Do others also feel the nervousness that has already started in the pit of my stomach, in anticipation and in fear of what will happen over the next 3-4 days. When the ocean decides that its ready to be approached will I be ready?

When its big and good, its hard to rush right into the water. I find myself observing the swell, my heart pounding inside my wetsuit, admiring what nature has created and wondering what it'll be like to get caught inside while paddling out. I wonder if I really want to do this, but everyone knows they will, for if we don't try it, you will always wonder for the rest of your life whether you could've cut on that day, whether you would have had the balls to take off, whether you could've made it out into the lineup.

On more than a couple occasions I've squandered the opportunity to get into some large quality surf by being out of shape, making the paddle out but being so fatigued I couldn't even paddle for a wave. This time is different, I've been surfing continuously for the last five months, I know I'm in good paddling shape so know its up to my head whether I'm really ready or not, do I have what it takes), not to impress anybody else, but just so _I_ know. Someday you'll hear people talking about the day it was soo big and so good and you know that you were out, you were there, and more importantly you surfed it. I don't know when I'll ever be in this situation again, that is being in shape, being at the beach and being young enough to still be able to try to prove things to myself and tests my limits. I know the time will come when I won't care to test my limits anymore, and it wouldn't be wise to, but when that time comes I'll be able to think back and say "yeah, I did it way back when" and be satisfied, not wondering. Everything else has been preliminaries, the main event is waiting to happen

OCTOBER 1982

I wonder how many other people are thinking this might be the swell, the one we wait a lifetime for. Are the others wondering what will happen when the wind finally turns offshore, cleaning up the raging froth the ocean has whipped itself into. Will we wake up one morning looking at 8 foot barrels peeling with machine like precision we only see in magazines. Do others feel the same nervousness that has already started in the pit of my stomach, in anticipation and in fear of what will happen over the next 3-4 days. When the ocean decides that its ready to be approached will I be ready?

When it's big and good, it's hard to rush right into the water. I find myself observing the swell, heart pounding inside my wetsuit, admiring what nature has created and wondering what it'll be like to get caught inside while paddling out. I wonder if I really want to do this, but everyone knows they will, for if we don't try it, you'll always wonder for the rest of your life whether you could've cut it on that day, or whether you would have had the balls to take off, whether you could've made it out into the lineup.

On more than a couple occasions I've squandered the opportunity to get into some large quality surf by being out of shape, making the paddle out but being so fatigued I couldn't even paddle for a wave. This time is different, I've been surfing continuously for the last five months, I know I'm in good paddling shape so now it's up to my head whether I'm really ready or not, do I have what it takes, not to impress anybody else, but just so I know. Someday you'll hear people talking about the day it was so big and so good and you know that you were out there, and more importantly you surfed it. I don't know when I'll be in this situation again, that is being in shape, being at the beach and being young enough to still be able to try to prove things to myself and test my limits. I know the time will come when I won't care to test my limits anymore, and it wouldn't be wise to, but when that time comes I'll be able to think back and think "Yeah, I did it way back when" and be satisfied, not wondering. Everything else has been preliminaries, the main event is waiting to happen.

This was written during an evening shift at the 84th Street Exxon in Ocean City, Maryland on Monday, October 25th, 1982. A massive Nor'easter was howling, over washing Route 1 in Delaware, flooding South Bethany and downtown Ocean City. Only a half dozen people came into the station that night – but we stayed open. Grammar was left "as it is" in this transcription. My paper was the backside of a station inventory sheet.

DREAM WAVE FOR THE ORDINARY SURFER

It was only a wave, but a brief glimpse many, many years ago, branded it into my brain. A mysto island point break, peeling left for an undetermined distance, with trails of backspray drifting in the offshore. The location was a mind-blowing surprise. How many others could possibly know about it – or have seen it when the conditions were just right? Not many I hoped. Someday, yes someday, I would surf that wave.

Sound familiar? But why do we always want something we can't have?

For most of us, dream waves break halfway around the world in some exotic, malaria-infested locale. Places like Bali, G-Land, or other god-forsaken unnamed Indonesian breaks where tigers make lunch out of your board bag. Or the more civilized Tavarua, where $4000 in airfare and wave reservations can go down the tube when the reef turns your back into hamburger.

Of course Hawaii is the land of dream waves, and lineups with 250-pound "bruddahs" who would like nothing better than to acquaint some naive haole with that unique version of the aloha spirit - a nice Hawaiian punch (in the mouth). Since only the most determined or wealthy surfers will reach these places, my sights are set a little lower. Which, believe it or not, leaves the wave I initially described still in the running. It breaks right here on the East Coast. Unfortunately (for me), many of you have seen it, breaking under the same conditions. And from what I'm told, it's even been surfed in recent years. So much for *The Endless Summer* fantasy.

But none of this lessens my attraction to it. For one, it doesn't break from East to West – you're actually moving in an Easterly direction when you ride it (a hint). Another thing is, when a Nor'easter has the coast in Victory-at-Sea conditions, this wave is clean. Offshore you might even say (another hint). And the wave is a tease, because even if you see it breaking, and your boards are on the car, you can't stop! (Well, theoretically you can, but just try and persuade the authorities it was an emergency.) The charge is trespassing, so you'll be out a fine, a towing charge, plus (hint, hint) the double-digit toll you just paid.

Have you Northeast guys figured it out by now? At the southern-most tip of Virginia's Eastern Shore is Fisherman's Island. When you're heading south on Route 13, the Chesapeake Bay-Bridge Tunnel crosses it right after you pay the toll. If you look to your left as the road turns out onto the bay, you'll see a point – and if the conditions are right, you'll slam on the brakes.

The first time I saw it was in the late 1970's just after a raging Nor'easter passed off the Virginia Capes. A buddy and I were heading to Hatteras, peering at the road through worn-out windshield wipers that were no match for the monsoon rains engulfing the Delmarva Peninsula. The drive had mostly been a blur, but the clouds started thinning as we got near the mouth of the bay. And like some divine sign, the sun came out when we paid the toll.

I was looking straight ahead as we started onto the 17-mile long causeway that would carry us over the white-capped bay – until my head suddenly lunged toward the dashboard when my buddy slammed on the brakes.

"Look at that!" he said.

"Huh? What, What?" I said.

"Over there – look!" he said, pointing out his window.

"Holy shit...."

A quarter mile away, peeling one after another off the point of Fisherman's Island, were perfect lefts. The size was hard to estimate from the elevated roadway, but the size wasn't important. It was the shape. Right here, in our own Mid-Atlantic backyard, was a legitimate point break.

But what made the wave even more amazing was that it broke on the backside of the island. Strong Northeast swells wrapped around the point to almost face back out toward the Atlantic, so the accompanying Northeast wind actually became offshore. Plumes of spray trailed each wave, and it wasn't hard to imagine the lines you could draw on such an inviting canvas – if you could only get to it!

A car came up behind us, but we didn't move. *Beep-Beep*. My buddy slowly let out the clutch so we could start to move forward. *BEEEEEEPP!* Okay, okay. Can't you see we're having a lifetime moment here? We drove off, but I kept looking back. My buddy adjusted his side mirror, but all he got was a good view of the guardrail. Soon Fisherman's Island was out of sight, but we took it as an omen for our trip. Yep, the waves in Hatteras were great. All three days' worth.

The memory of this wave has never faded away, although I wonder if I haven't embellished some of the details over time. You know, turned it into an East Coast (albeit reverse image) Jefferies Bay. But then again, for me, it might as well be Jefferies Bay.

So I've made up mind. If I ever see it breaking again I'm going to surf it – the fine, towing, and toll, be damned. It's got to be a hell of a lot cheaper than flying to Fiji.

* Originally published in Eastern Surf Magazine.

DEVIL BOARD

The fate of the board was probably sealed as I handed over my cash. Fleetwood Mac was at full dirge on the surf shop stereo, with Stevie Nicks gurgling indecipherable post-Rhiannon new-age mysticism about the "Sisters of the Moon." I don't know how many spinning sisters cast a spell on that late October afternoon, but it was karma all right – instant and bad.

The place was Virginia Beach, and I was on the way home from the worst Outer Banks trip I'd ever been on. I was looking for a winter board, something a little thicker and a little longer for the coming icy months, and had no doubt I'd find it among the many boards in the Swell Sliding Stick shop (name changed to protect the innocent – whoever they may be). The sales dude rattled on about the super late radical takeoffs he saw in Hawaii the previous winter, and steered me toward their new line of single/twin fin combo boards. Mark Richards I wasn't. I needed basic wave transportation, and settled on a clear, 6'4" single fin, double wing pin tail, with a distinctive half inch stringer – or what I now realize was…THE BOARD FROM HELL!

It was christened in December on a trip that included picking up a friend in Pottstown, Pennsylvania, then traversing the length of Philadelphia's dreaded Schuylkill Expressway during morning rush hour. The journey ended at the windswept Brigantine Jetty, where lines of clean calf-high crumblers mocked our surfing souls. We headed to a surf shop to wait for the tide – or a miracle – and caught the proprietor between tokes. He got an uncontrollable fit of the giggles when we decided to go out anyway, and I must say, his derision was well deserved. I got the longest ride of the day, going "low-and-slow" for almost five feet before my fin caught the bottom and gave me a chance to compare the taste of Jersey sand to Jersey tomatoes. Yeah, no contest.

The board got another chance in April, when it traveled with my new girlfriend and me to Hatteras for spring break. On a rainy, overcast, northeaster low-pressure morning, I paddled it out at Frisco – and got stuck. Months of collegiate elbow bending had me in dreadful paddling shape, so my arms were worthless by the time I made it to the line-up. I couldn't even catch a wave to get in. As I drifted toward Ocracoke, my girlfriend dutifully followed along with a tripod and camera, not knowing how much trouble I was in. Finally a cleanup set pushed me in, and I played dumb.

("Yeah, some days you just can't catch'em...")

So the next day I paddled out at the Lighthouse – and did the same damn thing! A flooded campsite topped off the trip, allowing us to experience the joys of car living for several days.

("Yeah, sometimes surf trips are like this…")

The board became the roommate board, and did its damnedest over the next several years not to be ridden. One roommate was on the verge of standing up when he stepped on a piece of glass while carrying the board to the beach. His foot healed, but his ego didn't, and he never surfed again.

My next roommate was incredibly game, though. I watched in horror and amazement as after only two weeks of surfing experience, he tried to takeoff on a tropical storm wave. He got to his feet and for a split second looked like Fred Flintstone, surfing on top of the wave instead of on the face of it. Then his board fell away, and he free fell down the green, six-foot face, into the mist of the churning pit. I paddled over to see if he was all right, and got ambushed. Jumping out of the foam like a fiberglass dolphin was the board, with a bulls-eye trajectory for my head. I deflected most of the blow with my arm, but the fin took a nine-stitch divot out of my scalp. Several weeks after driving me to the emergency room, my roommate went back to school – and never surfed again.

The board was retired, but not gotten rid of, and three years later, made its way to the Outer Banks again. My wife (formerly the girlfriend who endured spring break in Hatteras), and my just-out-of-the-Navy cousin, decided to paddle out with me on a seemingly small day. It was an easy paddle, but when I reached the lineup and turned around, my wife was the only person following me. My cousin was on the beach waving at us (seemed he'd spent enough time at sea). I was breaking in a new 5'10" thruster, which I'd bought at the same Virginia Beach surf shop as...the board that was floating my wife. She tried to catch the first wave of a chest-high set – and missed. With the next wave bearing down on her, she screamed for guidance. "Keep the nose up, and let the whitewater push you in," I told her. I guess she tried, but all I saw were her feet, and the tail of the board sticking out of the back of the wave. Then her feet disappeared, and the board shot straight up in the air, maxing the leash. She was in trouble, and even if she wasn't, I was.

I rode the next wave in, and just as she dragged herself up on the beach, I dove for her board, which was trailing behind. I missed, and the whitewater rammed the board into the back of her legs, taking her down with a thud. As I pulled the board off her coughing and twitching body, I realized that "small" was a relative term.

The board was mothballed after that, becoming dated and worthless in my basement – until last summer. A friend, who had been out of surfing for several years, was looking for a board. I let him borrow the board for a weekend, and when he returned stoked (and in one piece), I told him to keep it. He squared the deal by getting my broken garage door fixed for free, and then set off for a week long Florida surfari. Apparently he had a great time – after liberating his car from the sand in Anastasia Park, and paying his fine for surfing too close to the Jax Pier.

Maybe I should get him a Stevie Nicks tour schedule.

* Originally published in Eastern Surf Magazine.

SOUNDS OF YANNI

The day started in dashboard-glow optimism, with both of *The Endless Summer* soundtracks queued up in the car's CD player. Our coastal sources told us the swell from tropical storm Chris was showing, and we should get on it early. We did, chasing the sunrise until we crossed the Route 90 bridge at 7:15 A.M. Several rooftop American flags snapped to attention in the post-frontal system WNW wind, and my mouth went a little dry as a small purple spot on the inside of my arm throbbed with each adrenalin-inspired heartbeat. We seemed to have everything we needed – morning offshores and a good swell.

After relieving our bladders of their 20 oz. Royal Farms coffee backwash, we checked the conditions at a street with a reliable sandbar. Opening the car door a half a block from the beach revealed the roar of the surf, and standing up to unwind our car-creaky joints let us see the backspray of the waves. It was a good swell all right. Probably too good.

Although my buddy can surf, he is still new to the sport, and had never seen anything like it. A solid overhead NE ground swell, breaking at least 100 yards out, with even bigger lurching sets that took your breath away. (I would have sworn I was on the Outer Banks.) The swell also came with a strong north to south current, and we watched a paddling surfer drift two blocks south on his way to the lineup. The waves were a little closed out, but with patience and a lot of maneuvering, there were incredible rides to be had. There was no way around it, though. Kevin wasn't ready.

And neither was I.

There was a time when I wouldn't have given a second thought to charging such conditions. Say fifteen, five, or hell, even two years ago. But a little over a year ago my life was altered dramatically. The throbbing spot on my arm reminded me, just in case I forgot. I'm mortal – I have limits I have to live within.

* * *

In the spring of 1993 I was diagnosed with hemochromatosis, the iron overload disease. Because of a faulty gene, my body has no iron-uptake regulation, and readily soaks up any iron I ingest. So by age 33 I had over ten times as much iron in my body as a normal person – or almost enough to set off an airport metal detector. Excess iron is deadly because your body stores it in vital organs like the liver and the heart. As the iron builds up it poisons the organs. They die – and so do you.

A liver biopsy in July of 1993 showed plenty of iron in my body, but fortunately, no organ damage (the liver shows the effects of hemochromatosis first). Then I moved on to the treatment, which in these days of MRI's and organ transplants, seems like a remedy from a medieval barber.

The most effective way to remove excess iron from the human body is by removing blood, and the standard hemochromatosis treatment is having blood removed on a regular basis (known in medical terms as a phlebotomy). In my case it was a pint a week. The Red Cross only lets you donate a pint of blood every fifty-seven days, and I was scheduled to do it every seven. A perfect treatment for an active person – and someone with a history of passing out when stuck with a needle.

The fall dissolved into a blur of weekly visits to the hospital, and by Christmas, I had had 15 pints of blood removed in 16 weeks. I wasn't even thinking about surfing. Actually, I could hardly think. If I bent over and stood up, I got a massive head rush, and going up a single flight of stairs left me out of breath. My triceps shriveled, my aerobic capacity disappeared, I had junkie tracks on both arms, and I was depressed. Damn depressed. But I was getting better. The extra iron was leaving my body.

I survived the winter and the spring by alternately dreaming of my first day back in the water, and feeling sorry for myself. Finally, in May of 1994, my haywire iron levels started looking normal. The bloodlettings were cut back, some strength returned, and on my 34th birthday, I went surfing again, catching a glassy, sedate, waist high summer morning. I was out about twenty minutes, caught five waves and was exhausted – but stoked. Super stoked. I made it back. It was like catching my first wave all over again.

* * *

Although it had been three weeks since my last phlebotomy, and I felt as strong as I had in a year, I knew it wasn't enough. Not for today. If I made it out, and that was a big IF, I'd crap myself while dodging the sets. I knew the guys out in the water had been waiting all summer for a swell like this, and a real surfer should have been chomping at the bit to get wet. There was a bit of a lull, and I looked for a route out. Maybe, just maybe, I could...get real. It always looks bigger when you're in the water, and this looked BIG from the beach. It was hard to make a final decision, but we did.

We would head north to see if the inlet in the state park held the swell any better.

The south side of the inlet was – well, flat, thanks to the wonders of beach replenishment. It usually works better on a south swell anyway, but to not even show on a swell like this was quite a testament to the human ability to obliterate nature. A quick look at the Northside showed three guys out in smaller, more organized conditions than we'd seen earlier. There was some bump on the waves because the wind was more northerly here, but the swell looked approachable. I couldn't rein in the "real" surfer within me. "Let's go out here," I heard myself say, and Kevin obligingly pulled into the parking lot.

It was a brisk wind for August, so the change into our wetsuits was done quickly. As I pulled my board off the roof, a sun-faded Pontiac Fiero pulled up with a chunky 20-year-old single fin pintail strapped across its trunk. I caught the driver's eye when he stepped out, and said hello. He acknowledged me, grudgingly, and then asked if we'd checked anywhere else. After I answered, our newfound friend – Kevin would name him Yanni thanks to his resemblance to the musician – continued the conversation. With himself so it seemed.

"Sheeeit. My friend was supposed to wake me up this morning, but he never called. I told him I'd be up by 6:00 A.M., but I didn't hear from him, so I went over his house, and woke the dog, the kids, everybody..."

I was chuckling along politely, but starting to lose the thread of the conversation.

"I figured he might be having the best sex he's had in three months you know, so I didn't want to bother him. Finally he calls and I say the surf report says eight feet, and he mumbles you know, says he can't go. Sheeeit."

At this point, I gave up trying to follow what Yanni was saying, but I kept smiling and grunting responses. Kevin waxed his board, trying not to pay attention. We were just about to hear the story of Yanni's old board, and another board he was trying to get rid of, when Kevin stood up, put his board under his arm, and said, "Ready?"

Was I ever. "See you in the water," I said to Yanni, and he smiled and waved. "Okay."

Kevin looked at me out of the corner of his eye. "What in tha' heck was he talkin' about?"

"I wish I knew. Well, then again, maybe I don't," I said.

We walked under the Route 1 bridge, watching a boat in the inlet carefully negotiate through the strong current and swells making their way into Indian River Bay. When we got to the beach, waves breaking over the end of the Northside jetty were the first things we saw. Then we saw an additional result of beach replenishment – a four foot sand cliff that dropped down to the waterline.

Waiting at the base of the cliff was a steep descent to the raging overhead shorebreak. Each wave ran up the slope of the beach, and up and over the cliff, spraying sand and water high into the air. Once down the cliff you were pretty much committed – so I committed when the cliff collapsed from under my feet as I stood on the edge. Kevin joined me voluntarily, and we waited for a lull so we could assault the ocean with maximum momentum. Otherwise we'd be shorebreak casualties in wetsuit body bags.

Kevin and I both aborted charges down the hill, and were pelted with sand and spray as we stood mesmerized by the heaving walls of water flinging themselves on the beach. I was having second thoughts, but then Kevin saw an opening he liked and made a kamikaze sprint for the water. As he and his board skimmed out to sea, a set approached, and a voice came from behind me.

"Oh no man, don't do that." It was Yanni, and I wasn't sure if he just started talking, or had never stopped.

"Watch out, man, watch out – sheeeit." Yanni gave a wave-by-wave call as Kevin got pushed precariously back toward the beach. "He ain't gonna make it. No man, look out, look out. Hold on...whoa."

Finally Kevin stroked past the set to the relative safety of the impact zone.

"Damn, that was close. Look out, ah – he ain't gonna make it out, man," Yanni continued. John Madden he wasn't. He was more like Howard Cosell, you just wanted him to shut up. He wouldn't, so there was only one thing left for me to do.

Charge.

I got good momentum from the downhill run and easily escaped the danger of the shorebreak – and Yanni's yammering. My paddling turnover rate settled into a relaxed mode, but quickly shifted into a long dormant overdrive gear. I pushed through some whitewater, trying to keep moving as the lactic acid pooled in my triceps, and the tendons in my shoulders tightened like a leash in a Waimea wipeout. Non-stop swells filled the horizon, but I kept paddling until my jaw dropped so low that my beard stuck to the wax on my board. Then I was there. Somewhere "outside."

"What do we do now?" said a voice, and Kevin's presence surprised me. I hadn't been paying any attention to who was around me as I sat on my board puffing like a freshly caught blowfish.

"Get our asses back in one piece," I managed to cough out.

We made a great pair – the big wave rookie, and the experienced, yet wheezing old geezer. This wasn't fun. It was breaking bigger and farther out than it looked, so it really was an accomplishment to have made it out.

Still, what in the hell was I doing out here?

"I'm gonna' try and get a wave and go in," I told Kevin. He nodded, and watched as I paddled for a wave – and missed. I missed another one, and just started paddling for the beach, uncaring of what broke behind me. A lucky peek over my shoulder revealed a lucky chest-high peak coming right at me, which I caught and rode until it backed off in the deep water near the beach. I hung off the side of the board trolling my feet for the bottom, but 10 yards from shore I was still treading water. Lifeguard class sidestroke brought me and my board within five yards of shore, but there was still no bottom. Two more waves passed by me and broke on the beach, then finally, my feet touched sand. With board in hand, I raced the next wave up the slope, desperately launching myself at the crest of the cliff.

Safety at last.

My heart pounded in my ears as I stood up on the beach, surveying my escape route. Kevin was closing in on the beach now, looking for a safe place to land, but an incoming shorebreak set delayed him. He floated over the first wave, then the second, and the third wave lifted Kevin so high that I got a direct look into the bulging whites of his eyes. A pause followed, and Kevin made his break for land.

"I thought I was going to end up in your lap," Kevin said after ascending the sand cliff to join me. We stood squinting at the Victory-at-Sea conditions, wondering what possessed us to go out. I shook my head, and started to chuckle, and Kevin joined in. We both started laughing, trying to burn off the excess adrenalin running through our bodies, but we couldn't stop looking at the waves (and Yanni, who sat by himself out on the horizon, presumably still chattering).

What possessed us, what were we thinking?

The answer was simple. We weren't. Fear is a great motivator. And the fear experienced in the water was nothing compared to another fear – the fear of being mortal.

We headed home with the sound of the wind competing with the somber tones of the Counting Crows – and few words. The next day Kevin would head for graduate school in West Virginia, and I would be back in the hospital having the 32nd pint of blood drained from my body in the last 52 weeks. Flooding my silence were vivid scenes of the past, because it was exactly 15 years ago to the day that I bid an unknowing final farewell to one of the best surf buddies I ever had. Life had been many things since then, and "kind" wasn't always one of them, but at least now, I understood the significance of such an occasion.

And I was grateful – even for a day like today.

SURF MAG REQUIEM

They sit on my shelf like decaying dog-eared corpses. Faded, scratched, and abused. Some are classic titles of surf literature, like *Surfer* and *Surfing*, but others read like an obituary page of East Coast surf magazines. *Surf*, *Wave Rider*, *U.S. Surf* – the flowers have long since shriveled on the graves of these publications. But I can't part with them. I've already made arrangements to will them to the *Eastern Surf* Reference Library (a milk crate on Mez's back porch) when it's time for the final kick out.

What could be so special about a bunch of magazines? Let me see if I can explain...

A long, long time ago, in a distant universe called the Seventies, they were all we had. Magazines. They were your connection to the rest of the surfing world. You scratched up your pennies, taped them together, stuffed them in an envelope, and sent them to some exotic address (Dana Point, San Diego, or Melbourne Beach) and waited for your surfing lifeline. Only *Surfer* came out on a monthly basis. *Surfing* was bi-monthly, while others came out quarterly, or whenever they had enough money to publish. Understand now, this was back in B.C. (before cable). Depending on where you lived, you might get five channels on the tube, and one was PBS. No videos or VCR's either. If you were lucky, one of your buddies had a movie camera. Then you could sit around on wintery Friday nights, staring at 8mm movie footage so grainy it could've been used for a Loch Ness Monster "In Search Of" special.

Usually shown on somebody's kitchen wall, these movies were definitely rated 3-B – three beers and they looked good (yeah, Bob and Doug said it first). Actually they didn't look any better, you just had enough of a buzz that you didn't care. Besides, the ant-sized apparitions moving across the gray and white lumps on the wall were only you and your buddies squatting through the mush of your home break. *Wave Warriors III* it wasn't.

Just imagine it. No surf videos, no *Surf Reports*, no Weather Channel, no surf hot-lines, no Internet surfing newsgroups, no *Surfer* Magazine on ESPN, no surf shows on local access channels...you get the picture. Or should I say we got the pictures. The state of surfing was gauged by what you saw at your own beach and what came in the mail.

What came in the mail was sacred. A casual balls-to-the-wall bottom turn by Lopez at Pipeline, the nose of Shaun Thompson's board just sticking out ahead of a watery curtain, or Buttons, with spray flying from his board and his 'fro, doing some outrageous layback move you never even dreamed of. Then there was the exotic. The lefts of Bali appeared in print in the mid-Seventies, and an unnamed right peeling against the backdrop of an Indonesian jungle was published in 1979. These were the first pictures of Nias. The green barrels and green land of New Zealand always got your mind and heart racing (no sharks either!), while Peru and Brazil got billing over Central America. Costa Rica was still a well-kept rumor.

But what got you drooling more than anything was an East Coast shot. Sometimes it was just a blurry B/W photo stuffed in the "Pipeline" section, or it could be something as stupid as an East Coast ad – you weren't picky. But there it was in print...a validation of your existence...an East Coast wave.

Occasionally the mags threw us a bone, which kept us turning over the same pages for months at a time. *Surf* magazine once ran a "Guide to the East Coast," and that issue is the most beat up, dog-eared thing I have. Color photos from New England, New York, New Jersey, and the Outer Banks – all in one story. Who could've imagined such an East Coast overload? A year later, *Surfing* put together a monumental six-page Hatteras piece, which included a full color page aerial view of the Lighthouse line-up (the photo credits were by some guy named Meseroll). Soon after that *Surfer* put an Outer Banks wave on its cover – with a visiting Australian pro surfer riding it. Do you think Wes Laine would have made the cover for a feature about Bells Beach?

Somewhere along the way *Surf* disappeared, but then in the early 1980's, *U.S. Surf* popped up on the scene. It was a beautiful bi-monthly mag that gave out some heavy East Coast coverage. Lots of photos, with almost exclusively Eastern stories. It seemed like we finally had a voice of our own. Unfortunately, not long after my subscription money went in, the magazine went under.

By the mid-1980's, *Surfer* was publishing an East Coast insert, and the state of surfing was available in the moving images of videos. The world of surfing shrunk in other ways too, as surf camps and guided surf tours made exotic locations less exotic. With cellular phones and surf hot lines, a surf check can be done from the car, or from under the covers, and with accurate surf forecasts, those "surprise" swells are even rarer than before. Of course if you don't have to work, and absolutely never want to miss any waves, get yourself a pager and connect with the wave pager service. Hell, who needs to live at the beach anymore?

These days, in a shrinking surfing world, maybe a photo is only worth 500 words. (I mean, who has time to actually come up with a thousand?) Yet it still seems to be the essence of surfing. A moment frozen in time, giving us the chance to put ourselves in a specific place, on a specific wave. The East Coast photo will always be special because there is a chance we were out that day too, or the day before, or maybe we've been out at that spot on a day that looked just like it. We know exactly how the surfer in the photo felt, so just for a moment, whether we're sitting on the couch or on the john – we're TOTALLY STOKED TOO!

Enjoy these shots that *Eastern Surf* has collected from our coast. After three years, and 24 issues, it's probably safe to put your subscription money in the mail.

* *Originally published in Eastern Surf Magazine.*

HANGIN' TEN IN THE HEARTLAND

My surfboards were already strapped onto the car by the time the first swells from a Category 3 hurricane started rolling into Florida. It was early September, the Atlantic hurricane season was just about at its peak, and this storm seemed poised to deliver another memorable swell to surfers all along the East Coast. Call it fate, but this was the moment I picked to go on my "surfari of a lifetime."

After a 12-hour, 800-mile drive, I would finally paddle my board into the waters of...Lake Michigan?

What can I say? Surfing the Great Lakes is something I've dreamed of doing since Farmer John's were the cutting edge of wetsuit fashion. And the Great Lakes are surfed on a regular basis. I even called a Chicago area surfer to get advice – and reassurance.

"I think you're crazy," said Lester Priday, a transplanted Australian who was co-director of the Great Lakes District of the Eastern Surfing Association. The Manly Beach native couldn't contain his laughter after hearing of my plan to drive from Maryland to Lake Michigan during the most active hurricane season since 1933. But then Lester reassessed my sanity and listed some of the positive aspects of a post-Labor Day journey. The summer vacation crowds from Chicago and Detroit would be gone, the water would still be warm, and potent wave-producing weather systems would just be getting active.

"Well, you might get some waves," said Lester, trying to sound upbeat. "But I wouldn't count on it."

I wasn't fazed by Lester's less than encouraging words – at least until I got to Toledo. The drive had lasted nine hours by then, and there were at least three more to go. The 24 oz. "big buzz" coffee I drank near the Pennsylvania state line was wearing off, the cream doughnut I ate was repeating, rush hour traffic was crawling, and all I could think was, "What am I doing in Toledo…with surfboards on the car?"

Looking off into the orange glow of the western Ohio skyline, I decided Lester was right. The trip was a crazy idea.

So crazy that it had to work.

While chasing a setting sun across Michigan on I-94, the theme from the original *Endless Summer* movie played in my head. Yeah, so there would be no balls-in-your-throat boat ride with a crew of toothless Indonesian fishermen, or a "death in the afternoon" checkpoint showdown with some banana republic security force. Hell, there wouldn't even be a Brew-Thru pit stop to fill my beverage needs.

So what? My destination was unique. Globally, and good ol' U.S. of A. unique. Not only was I headed for the West Coast of Michigan, I was headed for the town of South Haven – the one and only "Blueberry Capital of the World."

Sitting on the shore of Lake Michigan in southwestern Michigan's Fruit Belt, South Haven had been only a "maybe" on my original itinerary. But Lester convinced me it was a worthwhile spot to check out because its location offered a relatively large swell window for the wave-producing low-pressure systems that move across Lake Michigan. South Haven also had a pair of piers to offer protection from the sideshore and onshore winds that are a reality of Great Lakes surfing. These piers, Lester explained, were actually long concrete jetties that could organize and shelter a precious freshwater swell from the usually less-than-optimal wind conditions. And on a really good day, the piers could produce clean East Coast-like inlet surfing conditions. (As an added scenic bonus, there was a prominent and still-working lighthouse sitting on the end of the South Pier.)

In addition to Lester's much valued surf advice, the South Haven Chamber of Commerce had sent me a guide describing the town as "a shining jewel on the Gold Coast of Lake Michigan." Having visited the Gold Coast of Florida, and lived in a condo on the Gold Coast of Ocean City, Maryland, I had already formed a mental image of this inland Surf City. But once I exited I-196 and started slowly cruising through the halogen streetlight blush of downtown South Haven, I could see that my speculative vision was completely wrong. There were no high-rises, and no neon strip of motels looming along the lakeshore. Instead, there was Phoenix Street – a sleepy tree-lined Midwest main street, with two barbershops, a bakery, a general store, a hardware store, a drugstore, and Bud's Optical, which had a pair of Green Giant-sized glasses hanging out front.

A typical surf town it wasn't...which didn't matter as long as there was surf.

In the darkness of the lakefront public parking area, I finally got a glimpse of the lighted South Haven Pier stretching out into Lake Michigan. It was hard to gauge the exact size of the short-period swells being pushed toward shore by a howling southwesterly wind, but some of them smacked loudly into the pier, sending spray up against the squat red lighthouse that sat on the end of the structure. There was no doubt about it, South Haven was a surf town. The only question was, would it still be a surf town in the morning?

It was. A still rising sun cast long maple tree shadows across the South Beach parking lot, while the brilliant blue sky over Lake Michigan was streaked with a brushwork of clouds. Best of all, the wind had died to a light breeze, allowing well-defined surging peaks to become glowing whitewater just out from the lighthouse. And I wasn't alone. Another surfer was already out enjoying the swells.

Since the Great Lakes have no tides to worry about, I decided to go grab some breakfast before hitting the water. But by the time I got back to the beach, this detour seemed like a mistake.

The ominous steel-gray clouds of a rapidly moving Canadian cold front covered up the sun, and the wind now blew out of the north at 25 mph, replacing the comfortable T-shirt temperature of earlier with a goose bump raising chill. Mini-sandstorms blew across the beach, and Lake Michigan's surface had turned an eerie green as it was strafed by wind gusts that guillotined the top of any wave that dared to stretch for the sky. The other surfer was gone too. Had I come all this way and blown it?

I scrambled into my spring suit, and found myself standing at the water's edge having an out-of-body experience. Part of my brain saw sand, water, waves, a jetty, and a lighthouse, and instantly screamed "Ocean!" Another part of my gray matter countered, "You're in Michigan; it's a lake, stupid." My sense of smell tilted the final verdict, alerting me to a crucial missing ocean element – salt air.

Other missing ocean elements would be sharks, jellyfish, and pinching crustaceans, but the lack of salt in the water was going to create a unique problem. A lack of buoyancy. Freshwater is about 20% less buoyant than saltwater, so even though I had brought a 7'4" there was a distinct chance I was under-gunned for the small salt-less waves. (A 7'4" surfboard minus 20% would be the equivalent of a board just 5'8" long).

Paddling out at a new spot is always strange, but my current surroundings were so unlike anything in my surfing experience…I might as well have been getting ready to paddle out on Mars. I watched intently as small, clean waves rolled in non-stop, leaving abbreviated trails of foam-less translucent whitewater in the shallow areas near the beach. Although these inside waves appeared too dumpy and weak to ride, outside near the lighthouse, tantalizing walls loomed up in distinct and recognizable sets. Only some of these walls had enough energy to spill forward and actually break, but "outside" seemed like the most promising place to start.

Once in the 70°F water, my board really didn't seem noticeably harder to paddle. And the water didn't seem any different than slightly turbid saltwater. It didn't take long to get outside, but it was obvious from an up-close-and-personal perspective that these waves were too mushy to ride. So I just sat there for a while, hoping for a "set of the day." It didn't happen. And I was uneasy. Not that I felt threatened by the conditions. Hell, I could see the bottom not far below my feet. Yet the scenery was just so stunningly unfamiliar…I was grasping to find reference points for my surfing instincts to cling to.

I decided to paddle back inside, looking over my shoulder with each stroke, finally stopping at a point that felt way too close to the beach. Surely my first wave would be nothing more than a skimboard ride with a face plant dismount. But while bobbing like a fishing float over the continuous swells, I started to see distinct sets. One set caught me by surprise and I got my first mouthful of Lake Michigan water. It went down like a 20-year-old bottle of scotch. Smooth. No burning or gagging.

Since I had been floating in Lake Michigan for a while now, I figured it was time to focus on what I drove 800 miles to do – catch a wave. On my first try I angled the board to cheat my way into the wave – and fell through the back. The same thing happened on the next wave, and the wave after that. Maybe, just maybe, I didn't have enough board for the conditions. Was I doomed to finish my Great Lakes surf session with a wave count of zero? ("You're craaazy, mate," echoed an Aussie-accented voice in my head.)

After taking a moment to regroup – I'd caught thousands of waves in my lifetime, surely freshwater waves were a riddle I could solve – I decided to keep the nose of my board pointed straight toward the beach during my next takeoff. If I ate Michigan sand, then so be it. At least it would be a low-salt snack.

Well, the next wave came (it actually looked like a real wave), I paddled straight, and much to my surprise, found myself being pushed toward shore. I quickly got to my feet expecting the worst, looked left, and got another surprise – there was plenty of wall in front of me. It was a small wall, but there it was. So I made a soft, deliberate bottom turn, lined myself up, and was "low and slow" by the end of the wave…and on the beach.

The waves then picked up a little, I got the place wired, and – damn! – all of a sudden I was having a blast. On Lake Michigan. I couldn't believe it. Good sets were thigh-to-waist high, but even the smaller waves had surprisingly good shape. Another surfer had shown up and was waiting at the waterline as I rode a set wave to the sand. Tanned and blond, he could've been the average surfer on any East Coast beach, but then he looked me in the eye and started walking toward me. I picked up my board and started approaching him. When we got within five feet of each other, he extended his hand. "Hi, I'm Craig Olsen," he said with smile.

I'm sure Craig had no idea how taken aback I was from our seemingly innocuous interaction. A traveling surfer has to be on their best behavior because most locals will view your presence as a threat to the local surfing order. I've learned that the best thing you can do is try not to be noticed – and not make eye contact. That way you won't see any threatening glances. Even along the relatively mellow East Coast you can feel a distinct chill when you paddle out at certain spots. Craig's enthusiastic waterline welcome was something I'd never experienced before in all my years of surfing. And I was grateful for it.

It turned out that Craig was a local from nearby Portage, Michigan, and was equally taken aback that someone would come all the way from the East for a surf session. But he was stoked by it too, as we shared waves and surf talk for the next half hour. Then another surfer made his way out to the lineup, and he and Craig began filling me in on all the different breaks along the lake. This surfer also knew the source of the set waves we were now enjoying. "There was a northern gale on the upper part of the lake last night," he explained. "These swells have traveled a couple hundred miles."

The lineup was so pleasant, like surfing with your buddies – waves and hoots for everyone. And just in case my surf surrealism gauge wasn't already pinned to overload, across the beach came a Kalamazoo television reporter. It turned out Craig had left a message for him earlier that morning. The reporter came to film the locals, but after he found out I was from Maryland, there was a two-minute feature on the Kalamazoo six o'clock news about the "Surfer who traveled to ride the lakes."

Shortly before noon the waves suddenly seemed to die – which I was told was a common occurrence. In the parking lot there was more surf talk, and offers of going out for coffee, but I was heading north to Grand Haven and needed to hit the road. As I pulled out of the parking lot, my new Midwest surf buddies and some just arriving windsurfers all stopped what they were doing to wave good-bye. I was almost too stunned to wave back. It's still one of my favorite moments of the entire morning.

While the surf on Lake Michigan may not be world class the vibe certainly was. Call me crazy, but I'm looking forward to going back.

Versions of this story appeared in the Washington Post, the Philadelphia Inquirer, the Chicago Tribune, the Orlando Sentinel, and the Kansas City Star.

SURF STUPID

I knew it was a stupid thing to do. Actually, it was a stupid thing to even contemplate, so going ahead and doing it would make me...the correct assessment here is, "reckless." Reckless and stupid. There's usually not a whole lot of good things happening when you pair these two words together.

And that's not all. If I had bothered to examine my idea closely, really taken the time to drag it out into the harsh light of day, I would have seen that it was flat out dangerous. But it was late afternoon in the rainy season. Instead of harsh light, there were only varied shades of gray.

So there I stood on the hard sand, a strange, sickly, sun-yellowed surfboard under my arm, contemplating paddling out into a totally empty and unfamiliar lineup. I was alone, thousands of miles from home, with only three people having a clue as to my approximate whereabouts on the globe. "Home" included my wife and my three-year-old son. If something unforeseen happened I would never see them again. It would probably be days before the locals even knew I was missing.

But still I stood there, staring out at a choppy gray Pacific Ocean. The sky was a similar shade, although it seemed to be fading to a dimmer wattage. At least this was the tropics, so it was almost a welcoming gray, not the I'm-gonna'-die-when-I-duck-dive Arctic expedition gray of a winter day in my home latitude. As the head-plus surf continued to crumble in long lines toward the shore, I pondered whether I was breaking most of the major surf travel rules, or just bending them a little.

Besides no one being out, and the rocks I'd seen earlier now fully submerged by the incoming tide, it turned out I was wearing a camouflage rash guard. For the moment, anyway, my slick new shark-gray top blended in almost perfectly with my surroundings. Math was never my strong suit, but the equation worked out something like this:

Gray Ocean + Gray Sky + Gray Rash Guard = The Invisible Surfer.

Yours truly.

A wave of clarity briefly washed over me. Just how far along the stupid continuum was I venturing? It wasn't like I'd taken a dinghy and puttered over vast stretches of open water to some mid-ocean cloudbreak. Even though I would be the only one out, I was still in a well-known Central American surf town that had become, at least for some, a little too well known. Certainly in the past I'd ventured beyond this axis point and survived. Coming to mind was the time I paddled out into 40°F double-overhead Hatteras Lighthouse after a four-month collegiate surfing sabbatical. (Oh yeah, I did that twice, didn't I?)

Yet for how many years had I dreamed about this moment? How many times had I imagined standing at the edge of the Pacific Ocean, poised to venture out at a break straight out of a surf magazine travel feature? How many times had I put myself in a magazine photo imagining this exact moment? (Honestly, my dreams were just a bit more inviting, but you get the idea.)

And of course there were my friends' firsthand travel surf stories, which I bravely smiled through while silently lamenting my lack of frequent flier miles. I'd always felt like I was behind on the surf travel curve – until this moment. Finally, I'd made it to one of surfing's Promised Lands. How could I not go out?

Because I knew better. Because I was a well-adjusted and responsible 38-year-old, not the naïve kid who first paddled out like he was attached to a giant kickboard two decades earlier. I had a wife, who had been part of my life for most of those twenty years, and a son whom I'd been Mr. Mom to for the previous three. They were the main reason I was here. When the chance to take this trip came up, they said I had to go. Of course their enthusiasm was based on the assumption that I wouldn't jeopardize my well being by…let's say, paddling out alone into an empty lineup thousands of miles from home.

Not that I wasn't supposed to surf. Well, actually I wasn't supposed to surf. But this wasn't because of any family issues. My wife understood completely that surfing in this country was a dream come true. No, the person who might not completely understand the "surfing thing" was my boss, who happened to be the editor of a D.C. area travel magazine. She was paying me a nice chunk of change – oh, did I mention the four-star hotels and the round trip First Class plane ride – to write about this burgeoning Central American golf Mecca that had a grand total of three golf courses.

How's that for a devil's bargain? You get a luxury trip to a world-renowned surf destination and your main priority is…golf. Yeah, I could've blown things off, but if I wanted more assignments just like this one, I had to deliver. Fortunately, my local tourist bureau contact wangled me an extra night on the country's West Coast (she definitely "got" it). But golf was the reason I found myself in this dilemma.

You see, I had arrived in town around 1:00 P.M. after a rain-interrupted round on a lush yet deserted layout somewhere in the middle of a nearby nowhere. The course's ex-pat American owner picked me up before breakfast, which I figured we would eat at the clubhouse. But then the heavens opened up, the owner's truck broke down, and the next two hours were spent captive in a sweltering maintenance shed awaiting the vehicle's resurrection. Somehow the sun came out, and by mid-morning we were miraculously at the course. Unfortunately, the clubhouse was a green construction trailer. No food, only sodas. By the time I hit town I had been up for eight hours and played 18 holes - on two cans of Pepsi.

It goes without saying that the waves were decent when I checked into the hotel. Despite the overcast sky and slight onshore wind, a small group of surfers were having a great time in the well-defined chest-high sets. What I wanted to do…what I wanted to do was rustle up a board and hit the water immediately. But the well-adjusted and responsible one – also the one with the throbbing head and slight equilibrium imbalance – reasoned that lunch was a better idea. So I watched the guys surf as I inhaled black beans and rice on the hotel's oceanfront patio. As soon as my queasiness lifted I hustled down a heavily-puddled dirt road to find a surf shop.

I'd barely gotten my fiberglass prize back to the hotel when the bottom fell out of the ominous moisture-laden clouds overhead. The winds came up too – not a soul was left in the water. A spasm of nausea almost double me over. Lunch had been fine, but I'd blown it. Blown it big time.

So up next on the agenda were several excruciating hours stranded in my hotel room watching torrents of water punish the palm trees lining the beach. How hopeless was it? My flight was leaving in the morning, and just a few days earlier it had rained liked this for 14 hours. Oh, man, I should've surfed right away. But hell, I could hardly stand up or rub two thoughts together. How could I be such an idiot? My one chance – had it passed me by? It was an afternoon of savage second-guessing, as this seemed like one of those regrets I would take to the grave. Then I noticed, or perhaps imagined, the rain and wind easing. Without a pause I stuffed my valuables into the safe, secured the room key on the loop in my trunks, and headed out the door.

Within moments the warm Pacific was rushing over my toes.

As the murky tropical water got thigh high, I knew I was a long way from the condo-lined and street-numbered Coastal Highway of my home break. With my thoughts locked into a loop of "this is my only chance" I floated my surfboard into deeper water, then hopped on to begin my paddle to the lineup. While pushing under the initial wall of rolling whitewater, a chilling summation froze my thoughts and knotted my stomach – I'd decided to risk my life rather than risk losing a dream.

Twenty years of surf magazine travel porn had taken its toll.

The lone crumbly wedge that I caught amidst my terrified state qualified as dream fulfillment in the sorriest way. But I did make it back to the beach in one piece. No one would ever know the level of stupidity and selfishness I achieved – and I vowed never to do anything like it again. I collapsed into bed that evening without bothering to have dinner, my overdose on surf madness leaving me in a deep, dreamless sleep.

Exactly why I was rewarded the next morning with brilliant sunshine, light offshores, and head-high A-frames, I'll never know. With a plane ride looming I was on it at daybreak, limiting my session to just over an hour. Yet it was enough to have me floating back to my hotel with an enormous involuntary smile etched on my face. As the Pacific Ocean ran down my nose, another much saltier liquid decided to mix in.

The Dream had indeed been fulfilled.

MOMENT

Idyllic – that's how this moment appears. Maybe even stretch it to perfect? Chris and I standing there making the trip's initial surf check. What more could we want than to scramble out of bed at sunrise and find this empty wave rolling onto "our" beach? It's the kind of moment that surfers everywhere dream about, right? Especially since all the cues point towards us being somewhere tropical. Surely the water is warm (it was), and there are coconut palms lining the beach (see the shell debris near our feet). After one quick look it was just a matter of running back to get the boards and paddle right out.

Well...

There's always a story behind the story. A picture can tell a thousand words – this one seems self explanatory, especially a number of years on. But squeezing tightly around the shiny wrapping paper of this idyllic morning was a gnarled ribbon of uncertainty that we were desperately trying to unravel.

For starters, we were all fighting off the hangover of the previous day's travel. Granted we hadn't crossed six time zones or dealt with a sketchy eight-hour South Pacific ferry ride, but it had been a sixteen-hour travel day including delays for a faulty Boeing 737 engine. This wasn't the ordinary wait at the gate delay while the plane got fixed. We had actually been taxiing out for take off when we suddenly turned around and headed back to the terminal. A disconcerting hour was spent stuck on the plane listening to the commotion of the left engine being disassembled, while an ever-concentrating and wholly nauseating odor of fresh jet fuel filled the cabin. Eventually things got quiet outside and the pilots attempted to restart the engine. When it "caught" they told us we were good to go…which was good, but we knew the expectation of a late-afternoon arrival surf session had vanished.

Our three-hour flight was spent readjusting our expectations and bleeding the smell of jet fuel from our nostrils. We slipped fortunately through customs with a minimum of hassle, braved the always bustling gauntlet of tourismo gauchos outside the airport doors, and found our ride. After a couple of stops, we didn't hit the coast until sunset, finally rolling through the gate of our accommodations well after dark.

So it was really only when we roused for the morning's surf check that our surroundings revealed themselves. This was our first stay at a property that we had booked sight unseen through the wonders of the Internet. Illuminated by the morning sun everything was new and unfamiliar, looking quite different than it did the night before when we'd closed the doors and shut off the lights.

Of course, shutting off the lights didn't mean we slept, as my room included the sounds of a gecko who resided in the hood over the stove. Rustling sounds in strange rooms on the first night of a trip are just a bit unsettling. So standing there on the beach, I was shattered. The shattering effect was enhanced by a lack of water, as we had all dutifully polished off our bottled supply the night before, determined to stay hydrated, figuring we'd have access to water in the morning. Now we were soaked in our own sweat by simply standing on the beach, and seemingly without an obvious potable water source. There were taps in the rooms but nobody was going to chance that on day one. Our host would be serving breakfast sometime in the near future, but at the moment food service was yet to be up and running. Naturally, as soon as you can't have something, that "something" is all you can think about. My mouth got exponentially drier with each bead of sweat that ran down my back.

With no water and no food service there was now a criminal lack of the one thing that would have helped de-shatter the morning. There was no coffee. For me, a longtime caffeine junkie, this incited more desperation than the lack of water. Dehydration, no sweat. Screaming adenosine receptors…I wanted to scream too. Words were coming out of my mouth sideways if they came out at all.

We did have provisions in the form of energy bars, which came with a Surgeon General-like wrapper advisory recommending that you consume them with plenty of water. The thought of choking them down dry left me with an image of The Three Stooges dressed in Civil War garb chewing on a "cake" that was actually a pillow.

(Moe: "Tastes like Southern Comforter…")

Finally, John, who took this photo, had emerged from his room covered with itchy red welts. He was bitten during the night in his bed, which seemed to scream "bedbugs!" The rest of us were silently relieved to have emerged from the night unscathed, yet there was a heavy cloud hanging over the morning. Was our stay at this place already over? If it was, we had a bit of a situation, as the night before at check-in we handed over six days worth of rent…in cash. How willing would the owners be to hand back $1200 and let us walk out of here? Like there was really anywhere else for us to stay in this throwback pequeno pueblo?

After walking back from the beach we all hovered outside of our doorways talking quietly. No one was waxing boards or lathering on sunscreen. If we needed to leave, we just wanted to get on with whatever hassle that process was going to entail. Plus, it didn't seem right to be thinking about surfing while John had what looked like a serious problem…that might affect us all.

Combining the travel fallout with the lack of water, lack of caffeine, lack of sleep, and the fact that several of us were now regularly dodging AARP mailers, it was hard to think of charging. Actually, it was hard to think, especially with the heat index seeming to rise by the minute. The one thing we were all thinking about, but not saying out loud, was this: Was our trip already doomed to be one of those trips where absolutely nothing goes right?

Our hosts were certain that ants, not bedbugs, had left the welts on John (he did admit to snacking in bed). They quickly agreed to swap out the mattress and the bedding, and sweep up the room. Whether that was really the solution or not, we went along with it. It was all we had the energy for. Maybe our optimism was misplaced, but we desperately needed something positive to grab onto. Then maybe that ribbon we were still tugging at could start to unravel.

With the morning now seemingly cleared of a major obstacle our thoughts turned back to surfing. Was it time to hit the water? Or did our bodily needs outweigh the desire, or maybe even our ability to surf?

A rock reef that we had surfed on a previous trip was just starting to show about a half mile up the beach (we had surfed but never stayed in this location before). Chris and Philippa were waiting on that wave, knowing it would be more user-friendly than what the pitchy beach break was offering. Waiting would also offer some time for hydration and sustenance, as we got word that the well-stocked local mercado was open.

Still, it was hard to wait, especially with a glassy wave breaking right out front. There was some discussion about whether it was just a tantalizing closeout, but it looked, at least to my travel-addled eyes, rideable if you were patient. With a few bites of Cliff Bar sawdust in my stomach, I tried to size up the scenario the best I could: waist-plus beach break, easy paddle, maybe a little zippy on the entry...manageable in my current state of torpor? Could three decades of surfing experience override the lack of caffeine, food, caffeine (yes, again), and water?

I volunteered for a reconnaissance mission. My son Andy got his induction notice a few minutes later, although he pretended not to hear me as he pulled the covers over his head.

The water was warm and clear as Andy and I waded in – welcoming for sure. As things got a little deeper I could see scurrying on the sandy bottom. Rays. While this didn't stop me in my tracks, I did start to shuffle my feet a little, looking quickly to get to paddling depth. It didn't take much to get out, and before we knew it we were bobbing in the intense tropical sunshine.

Since we had declined to give the airlines an extra $500 on this trip, our boards were rentals. Yet mine was no standard issue rental – it was a brand new board. And it was already lending some optimism as I could tell from how it paddled that it felt "right" (by the end of the week I wanted to take it home). Then, finally looking back toward the beach, the slow motion fog that surrounded me all morning quickly burned away.

Rising in the distance above the coconut palm canopy lining the beach were coffee-colored mountains whose mile-high peaks played hide-and-seek with slow drifting clouds. Far off to my right (East), the coastline curved out to a familiar headland, while just up the beach to my left, a few surfers were now populating the rocky reef that served as the area's main break. We had an audience too, as Chris, Philippa, and John huddled under the shade of some juvenile almond trees that sprawled their bushy cluster of leaves close to the ground. Being all good friends the pressure wasn't really on, but I certainly didn't want to blow my first wave. We needed all the positive karma we could get. (Yes, making the first wave wouldn't hurt my ego either.)

Andy's rental, while made of indestructible epoxy, was proving to be as maneuverable as a garage door. The brand of the board was one that had never impressed me, so I wasn't surprised. I would have gladly given him the first wave of the trip, but this board was going to give his burgeoning surf skills all they could handle. His first wave was going to fall into the "work in progress" category. (Fortunately, progress came quickly in later sessions on a very different and much more rideable board.)

So christening the trip, and maybe setting the tone for things to come, was up to me. It was joyful to float over the glassy peaks that rolled with a clockwork regularity toward the shallows inside. There was just enough juice, nothing happening outside to keep us on edge, only the sun, the clear water, and whatever I could still see making sand trails on the bottom. I was in no hurry, patiently waiting for just the right left to come my way. It finally did, and I set about stroking my virgin board for the blue-green wall rising behind me.

The board paddled like a dream, catching the wave easily. I set up mostly straight, and upon standing up, landed my feet in just the right spots to feel completely at one with the board. Together we planed smoothly down a larger wave face than I anticipated, and with hardly a thought, I leaned the board over on its rail for a quick turn off the bottom. Any questions or mistrust I had melted instantly as I effortlessly pointed my fiberglass partner's rounded nose back up towards the lip for a satisfying roller coaster climb-and-drop to pick up speed. The wave face turned green thanks to the backlighting of the sun, and I could see the bottom rushing by as I managed to squeeze in one more quick pump before kicking over the top for a textbook finish. Looking back at the beach, there were double-arm waves of approval and thumbs pointed toward the sky.

Our unwanted ribbon had finally begun to unravel. It turned out to be anything but one of those trips.

COFFEE AND CREMAS

There's not a hint of sun in the sky, yet somehow the roosters in the next yard have been in full voice for the last 45 minutes, adding their throaty lead vocals to the ambient drone of the ever-running air conditioner. It's questionable as to how much sleep I've gotten, or whether I've really gotten all that I needed. It doesn't feel like it. There's a bit of soreness in my ribs and shoulders as I try to sit up and put my bare feet on the cool stone floor. But I was expecting to feel much worse. I need to make a note to pat myself on the back for all the miles covered in the pool and on the road. There were also hours spent in the musty basement doing a core-based resistance workout. It's all added up to perhaps a shape I haven't touched since my twenties. Undoubtedly, the healthiest surf trip I've ever had. Which is saying something for someone halfway through a fifth decade of life.

With a barely audible "click" the small lamp on the bed table throws a shadowy glow onto the curtains and wood paneled walls, allowing me to stand up and feel the sand that's been tracked into the room. It does get swept every day, but it's hard not to bring sand inside every time the door opens.

A few deliberate steps and I'm at the door, fumbling with the switch to light up the compact kitchen area. After accidentally turning on the outside light – ah, I'll just leave it on, then Chris will know I'm up – I hit the correct switch and a bare compact fluorescent bulb high in the ceiling emits a ghostly metallic hue. It's not all that bright but still hard on the eyes (nasty little things). The coffee maker already has water in the reservoir and a filter sitting in its basket. Mastering such details at 5:20 A.M. can have a groggy slow motion Mt. Everest summit camp feel…or at least what I imagine that altitude would feel like. In taking care of these things the night before it feels like no precious pre-dawn moments are wasted.

Completing the morning requires only one more thing – opening the plastic gallon-sized baggie that holds the coffee and other perishable foodstuffs. On my first trip to this still wondrous country I was schooled by a local about the ubiquitous "little black ants." They are everywhere, in every structure, always looking for food. Leave a crumb on your floor overnight and you'll have an ant trail a mile long. Yeah, you can always clean your mess, but they'll be checking back on a nightly basis…for the rest of your trip. By keeping all food stuffs in plastic from minute one of your check-in, you can get through your trip with a minimum of Insetca-Mammalia skirmishes.

A quick slide of the plastic lock lets a wondrously sweet and bitter aroma waft out of the bag and into the room. It is, to my nose, and the olfactory bulb buried deep inside my gray matter, the aroma of the gods. With just a single whiff I know exactly where I am in the world – there is only one place where I've experienced this magical co-mingling of fragrances. My heart automatically speeds up, as through the years this smell has conditioned me to expect that the coming day will be: 1) a good one, 2) a great one, or 3) one that will be etched into memory until my final days.

Thanks to a tattered and yellowing psychology degree, I know that a smell-generated sense memory can be powerful and long lasting. In addition, they are typically vivid and emotional – as my pre-dawn research just confirmed. So for good measure I stick my nose over the bag, inhaling deeply, hopeful that if there ever comes a future point when the travel required for this exquisite snort is beyond my capabilities, somewhere in the distant recesses of my neurons, this moment and this feeling will be a "permanent record." That somehow I'll always be able to find my way back to it even as other recollections melt away.

Here's to Coffee and Cremas.

.

Chris Tousimis

THIRTY-TWO YEARS TO ESTERILLOS

Although a Rip Curl "Live The Search" team had recently chased Seven Ghosts, we were only looking for two. And the foggy apparitions in question were the teenage-selves John and I had been one summer thirty-plus years earlier, when the surfing bug bit both of us, and the unseen hand of karma conspired to have our paths cross in a bustling beach resort crab house kitchen. The chase, as it stood now, didn't involve trauma surgeon-approved tow-in waves, or days of sketchy travel to the most remote outposts of the known surfing world. Even though both of us had been fortunate enough to reach the decade of "five-o" in good health and just a few pounds past the trim of our youth, we had a sturdy grasp on our current abilities. A welcoming and well-worn Central American destination with glassy head-high waves, air conditioning, and Wi-Fi offered the perfect comfort level for the occasion.

For the moment, the chase was on pause as John and I sat in the channel trying to shake off the inevitable physical fallout of squeezing seven intense surf sessions into a 72-hour period. The world class beauty of our surroundings – lush green-covered hills behind us, a coconut palm-lined beach curving to our south for miles, an intense tropical sun aimed directly at our foreheads – probably masked the true depths of our fatigue, although my throbbing ribs left no doubt that the morning's double dose of Advil had worn off. But our well-earned breather had intent that went beyond the physical. It offered us a moment to reflect on the trip, and everything else that led to us being here on this postcard perfect morning in Costa Rica.

Obviously, our history went back a long, long way. That John and I were both still surfing and still surfing together after all these years was quite an achievement. It had been a challenging journey, complete with many periods when it seemed that the two of us had better odds for time travel than we did for ever achieving this shared state of exhaustion. Numerous were the personal threads connecting our lives at this point, but the big one, the thread that made our present-day travel situation extraordinary was this: Once upon a time, John and I shared a five-hour car ride to Cape Hatteras, North Carolina. Not only was it our first surf trip together, it was also the first surfari either of us had ever taken. Now, after 32 years, our second surf trip together had finally become a reality.

That first surfari had served as a giant exclamation point to a now distant and storybook summer. Joining John and me on that trip were two other deep-fryer mutineers who also didn't bother to stick around for the final overtime-laden work shifts of late August. Between magical thinking and dumb luck we scored the best waves we had ever seen, which by coincidence, we finally had enough skill to enjoy. We also captured the essence of our summer during an afternoon siesta at the Cape Point campground. In a moment of blind inspiration we put our 35mm Minolta on a tripod, set the self-timer, and took a picture – all four of us lined up, boards in the foreground, the Lighthouse carefully centered between us, while a T-shirt with "Cape Hatteras" in large yellow letters was held up for our Kodacolor to capture (see page 25).

A few days later we packed up our Maryland beach apartments and scattered to our respective colleges. But the trip lived on in that photo, which ended up carefully tacked to the bulletin board overlooking my desk. Any time I glanced up from a textbook, our glorious moment in the sun stared back. The journeys we took that fall, at least in my mind, were epic. There were the obvious surf destinations like Hawaii, Mexico, Australia, and New Zealand, but this was a time when Naughton and Peterson were inspiring surfers to "Centroamerica" and other venture-to-guess destinations. Bali was officially part of the surfing vocabulary, as was Java and Fiji, and a mysterious Indonesian right had recently landed a two-page color spread in *Surfer* (it was Nias). There was a big world out there, and I was determined to see it from a surfboard. Prayer-inducing closeouts, treacherous dugout boat trips, malaria pills, festering reef rash, dental floss-stitched gashes...count me in. Or at least I'd like to think I was in. Such was my faith in our surfing inspired friendship.

Yet a funny thing happened on the way to the passport office. Our surfari had ended with the unspoken yet implicit premise that we would all return to the beach the following summer and pick up right where we left off. Unfortunately, only two of us made it back, and it was quickly apparent that one of us was a very different person from the summer before. Our world conquering surfing foursome had dissolved into the sands of reality.

(To a culture currently addicted to instant feedback, our lack of planning and communication must seem "quaint." But there was a time when friendships, even close ones, were kept and continued during extended periods of little or no contact. A couple of things contributed to this, especially if you were male. For starters, guys didn't write letters to other guys. A postcard maybe, but a full-on letter with stationary, stamp, and envelope? Nope. Rarely happened. The other thing was that long distance phone calls were crazy expensive. And in addition to the expense, one of the least reliable forms of communication ever invented was the dorm-to-dorm long distance pay phone call.)

This unfortunate demotion to solo surfer status was a cold slap of life that lingered for a while. I continued surfing, coexisting with roommates who had a passing but not a hard-core interest in the sport. Several got an A for effort, but surfing never offered them the same adrenalized fix that my body somehow extracted from just carrying a board to the water's edge. With early morning interest leaning more towards catching Z's than waves, I was usually alone and scanning the lineup for any sign of John or the other two lost surf crewmembers.

By the mid-1990's I'd somehow become not only a writer, but also an at-home dad with an infant son. It was right at this time that a prominent children's magazine – the one found in doctor's offices everywhere – wanted to know if I could come up with a surf story. After some thought, I condensed, cleaned-up, and slightly fictionalized an account of that first surfari, prominently featuring John, as he and I had shared an epic window of peeling left-handers while the other half of our group was checking out surf shops. (John and I were the fortunate goofy-footers of the foursome.) Once I received the advanced galley of my story I decided that after 17 years, I should really try and find John. At the least, he should know he was in print.

All it took was a two-minute call to John's alumni office and I was staring at an address and a phone number. It was stunning, really, and even more stunning was the fact that John lived just 20 miles away. I composed a letter – what else would I do as a writer – and sent off a copy of the story. Within a few days I got a phone call. It was John. It definitely sounded like John. The voice, the upbeat demeanor, all just as I remembered. And he was still surfing. Since we were both a bit inland at this point, a day trip was arranged to surf and get reacquainted.

In looking back, this trip was an enormous risk. We'd known each other for just a few short months many, many years ago. Daily surf sessions and a shared surfari did give us a deeper bond than the average seasonal beach acquaintances, but after 17 years we were essentially strangers. If we found each other vastly changed from how we remembered – and there was already precedent for this – it was going to be a very long day.

Early in the drive I was nervous. Hell, it was almost like a first date. But we weren't on the road long before it hit me – time had stood still. John was John. He was exactly the guy I remembered. We had some catching up to do, but once in the water it was like no time had passed at all. In fact, it could have been simply the next summer. The waves weren't that great but it didn't matter. John and I had reconnected. Best of all, the day felt like a beginning, not the desperate dead-end nostalgia trip that over-the-hill jocks take during last call at a class reunion. It turned out to be about much more than just waves.

One thing our outing didn't do was to rekindle my now ancient travel dreams. They'd never come close to being fulfilled. I'd certainly had plenty of domestic surfari's, including one to the "exotic" shores of Lake Michigan, but thoughts of grander destinations had floated off over time like untethered helium balloons. With a ten-month-old at home and a writing career that was just climbing out of startup mode, it was hard to see beyond diapers and deadlines. That John and I had been able to again surf together...that was good enough.

John then met the family, and in many ways became part of the family as we managed to share some great days of surfing over the next year. Eventually though, the issue of travel reared its head – with John. I like to think I had some influence on his decision to ditch real life and travel the world for nine months, but he had already done some serious traveling before our reunion. The difference for his travels this time was that surfing was his main motivation. John was ever the loyal friend, sending regular e-mails from Internet cafes around the globe recounting his latest excellent surf adventure. Bali, Fiji, Australia, New Zealand, Hawaii – he surfed them all. Somehow his messages had a knack for arriving just after a diaper change. Just in case I didn't realize that our lives were worlds apart in ways that transcended geography.

To say I wasn't jealous would be a lie to make a politician

proud. I tried to salve my feelings with the fact that one of us had made it. That was better than none, right? I thought so until John stopped by after his travels and covered my living room floor with photos, pamphlets, and souvenirs from his trip. Looking hard at John's collection...I knew I wasn't getting to those places anytime soon. So a fun afternoon quickly turned bittersweet as I wrestled with the notion that I was too much of a jealous prick to be totally awed by John's incredible journey. Oh my God, couldn't I just be happy for the guy? Couldn't I get "me" out my head for a couple of hours? I tried, but all I could do was question my own status as a surfer. Did I even qualify to call myself a surfer? After almost two decades in the sport, I still hadn't really "traveled." And at that moment, I couldn't convince myself that I ever would.

The best way to describe what happened a few weeks later is with a classic line from Casablanca: "It seems that destiny has taken a hand." On my answering machine was an editor, a desperate editor at that, who needed a golf article. The catch was, instead of being about the local driving range or miniature golf course – my previous work – this assignment required some travel. All the way to Costa Rica, first-class airfare and lodging included. While the golf was good, the surf was even better. That first paddle out with John after I got home was pretty special. We were both "real" surfers now.

For the new millennium John and I moved into that phase of life where time speeds up, and the only certainty seems to be change, often major change, no matter how hard you try to avoid it. We both continued surfing, although our phases of balancing life and surfing didn't always align. Sessions together got a bit sparse, with my connecting thread often being a phone call or email from John telling me how good it had been. Occasionally, I was the one doing the telling, but not very often.

Fortunately, our communication never flagged, and there was always talk of travel. John was landing one significant trip a year, while I leaned heavily on family outings to the Outer Banks. Mutual invitations were always given, but again, we just couldn't align our schedules. To celebrate the 30th anniversary of our Hatteras surfari, we did have a memorable surf at our home break – exactly 30 years to the day, even on the same street where we learned together all those years ago.

A day later I left for the Outer Banks, and something about those two events inspired me or scared me, I'm still not sure which. But surfing moved back up the priority list. My water time increased dramatically, even to eagerly taking on our mid-Atlantic winter surf again for the first time in years (gotta love 7mm mitts and booties). This recommitment rewarded me with one of my all-time favorite sessions, coming on a New Year's Day after Santa left a new quad under the tree. With only John, my son, and another good friend in the 38°F water, I christened the board at a secret sandbar that had recently formed in front of a private "no access" community of unoccupied multi-million dollar beach houses.

I was indulged by my family to celebrate my 50th birthday in Costa Rica, and just nine months later, John was planning to do the same. Again my family indulged me, agreeing that it was time for John and I to finally take that trip. Maybe it would be a year or two before we paid off the credit card – especially after two Costa trips in a year (is that even allowed?) – but it was an opportunity that might never come again. Such sentiment might strike some as too heavy, too somber, too...maybe even too pretentious. But life happens, often before you realize it. Putting things in perspective, it had been 32 years since our first trip – if I added 32 years to now, where did I end up? Someplace I really didn't want to think about.

Thankfully my ribs didn't hurt much as John and I smiled and laughed while recalling our first trip, speculating that "those guys" probably would have chanced the enticingly glassy yet thoroughly closed-out overhead waves that were blasting the board shorts off the well-tanned and nimble crew trying to surf in front of our hotel. Ambitions among our group of age-enhanced surfers were a bit different. We'd loaded up the rental and driven 20 minutes to a rock reef that not only turned the swell into defined peaks, if you connected your sections just right, the rides were incredibly long. Besides a friendlier wave, the 20-minute drive also served to turn the clock back at least 20 years as the town where the break was located still held an endearing low key and local vibe. A glance toward shore offered us a taste of what most Costa Rican beachfronts would have looked like if we'd taken this trip decades earlier.

But decades earlier I doubt that I would have been humble enough to abandon a standard thruster for a longer and rounder egg shape that was much more attuned to the less-critical faces the rocks created. In merging board and break – I think it's called experience? – I'd been rewarded with the longest wave of my life, a right that went on and on and on, then became a left, and then reformed back into a right before finally depositing me near shore where the rocks gave way to sand. On a single wave I had made more turns than I might during an entire session at home. Following my progress the whole way was John, who was still on the beach stretching out his back.

Gently bobbing in the Jacuzzi-temp water, watching sets form over the nearby reef, talking with John...it was a movie I'd played in my head thousands of times, especially in our younger days. Yet it just didn't seem real. Not that it was a dream, either. It was something otherworldly – the otherworldly quality no doubt owing to the fact that our moment had been more than three decades in the making. Throw our 17-year hiatus into the mix, and it was a moment that spent a long time outside the boundaries of possibility.

But here we were, at a time in life when you don't openly admit but have internally conceded that dreaming is a young person's sport, and some of my longest held dreams were being knocked out left and right. Stack seven surfboards precariously on the roof of an SUV and trundle down a narrow, dusty, crater-filled dirt road searching for surf? Check. Glass-off, orange-glow, Pacific sunset session with a group of friends? Check. Watch John bravely and expertly take off on the biggest wave I've ever seen him on? Check. (The cost for my in-the-pit perspective of the ride? A thundering wall of whitewater, complete with double spin-cycle. Priceless.) The longest ride of my life with my original surf buddy present to witness, verify, and celebrate? Check.

"Well, we did it," I managed to croak out while trying to keep my voice from cracking. John smiled and nodded. "Yep, we sure did." No hype was needed. Few moments in my life have felt so pure.

I thanked John for not only asking, but also for gently encouraging me to make the trip, then caught an uneventful wave and went in. After weaving my way through the thoroughly local Sunday beach crowd, I made it to the truck where Philippa stood with a smile and that distinct post-surf-zen look in her eyes. The others on the trip, and this also included Chris and Pere who were still in the water with John, had previously been the most casual of acquaintances. Yet we quickly morphed into a fun yet dedicated ensemble that was all about the surf – early to bed, early to rise. Rather than spending late nights over Imperials and Pilsens, the rising sun and offshore mornings were our time of celebration. This morning had been no different. We caught the swell, wind, and the tide just as we'd hoped. It was more than a good morning; it had been a glorious one.

Philippa and I watched the surf, although with the break being so far out and the sun slightly in front of us, it was almost impossible to make out any details of the surfers left in the water. After a bit we saw a rider on a nice chest high left, although we couldn't tell whether this individual had his left or right foot forward. Soon it was clear that the surfer was in fact a goofy-footer, and as the wave continued to link with the next section, he cut back and took it right. The surfer continued, getting closer and closer to the beach, finally coming left, straight, and then left again as the wave finally gave out. It was the longest ride I had seen all morning. At this point our surfer mixed in with a group of backlit swimmers and disappeared. But it wasn't long before I saw John walking up towards the truck, looking like he'd won the lottery.

"That was you?" I asked. My question was implicitly understood.

"Yeah, that was me!!" John answered with a laugh.

Just hours away was the cab ride ending my trip, yet I didn't feel sad at all. Not being here – now that would have been sad. At the moment, so much had been accomplished, I felt so alive...like the endorphins and adrenalin of a 19-year-old were coursing through my body. It was a final session that I would have never dared dream up, and like the magical afternoon John and I shared long ago in Hatteras, one I will never forget.

And what of our ghosts, the ones trapped in that campground photo and in the children's story? We never actually found them, although John and I were certain that they would be proud of their elder surfing selves. But we did find something they left behind for us many years ago – the promise of that first summer. We fulfilled it every time we paddled out into the Pacific. It was a simple yet exquisite gift. Each morning held the exact same promise as those distant mornings of our first surfari: a beautiful day, fun waves, with the chance that this might be the best day of surfing...ever.

Earl Shores, Chris Tousimis, and John Doub. Costa Rica.

ACKNOWLEDGMENTS

A personal thank you to all of the friends who have been part of this "surfing thing" through the years. You may not have realized it at the time, but you were helping fill the pages of this book.

The following paragraph is ordered chronologically. Andy Brown: Thank you for passing on your stoke and knowledge during the Phillips' "Summer School" of 1979. John Doub: Thanks for your ever-present upbeat attitude and for sharing so many of my all-time surf moments. Harry Brubaker and Jack Wainwright: What an epic summer, what an epic trip – without it, I may never have written a single word. Greg Cruciano and Wally Slagle: Thanks for the great times in and out of the water and for being friends I could always count on. Steve Hawk: Your encouragement and praise of my early work meant everything, without them this book doesn't exist. Dick Meseroll: I'm forever grateful, as my writing career – now like *Eastern Surf*, a quarter century old and counting – was launched because you took a chance on "some dude" from Maryland. Loree Lough: Thank you for your encouragement, your guidance, and for welcoming me into the writing world. Paul S. Newman: It will always be an inspiration that a writer of your stature enjoyed my work. Lee Gerachis: Thanks for always making me feel welcome, and for all the sublime surfing advice. Kevin Brittingham: Timing is everything, still grateful to this day for our surf sessions. Rob Beedie: That beautiful board is perhaps the ultimate compliment my words have ever received.

To my current day travel crew, there's just not enough space. John "El alcade de Esterillos": Can you believe we're still going 37 years later? Chris Tousimis: A special "Thank You" for letting me use your amazing art (title page and page 96), and also for the zen dawn patrols, the Crema awards, and for sharing my sunrise 1820 "rocket fuel." Philippa Hughes: Grateful to our knack for exchanging "best wave" sightings, writing thoughts, and observing how on most days in the lineup, you're braver than the guys.

Michael Kronenberg: So grateful for your very personal contributions to the book. The cover is beautiful. It starts telling the story before a single page is turned.

And to my family…thanks for living with my surfing obsession for all these years. Not only has Robin put up with surf travel and spent chunks of her life on beaches (both freezing and sweltering) with a camera in her hands, she has also spent decades reading my surf writings – which, in the beginning, weren't very pretty. To Andy, who was born into this world with unsaid and wholly unfair ocean expectations – his birth announcement appeared in *Eastern Surf* – yet ended up becoming a surfer anyway. Finally, to mom, who made me wait until I turned 18 to get a surfboard. Delayed gratification can end up being a beautiful thing.

PHOTO CREDITS

ABOUT THE AUTHOR

Earl Shores is a former Contributing Writer to *Eastern Surf Magazine*. He has written about sports and surfing for publications ranging from *Highlights For Children* to *Sports Illustrated*. In addition to *Surf Lessons*, Shores co-authored *The Unforgettable Buzz* (2013), and *Full Color Electric Football* (2015).

For more information about the author and his work:

www.earlshores.com

www.fullcolorelectricfootball.com

www.theunforgettablebuzz.com